T0316599

Cambridge Elements

Elements in Campaigns and Elections
edited by
R. Michael Alvarez, Emily Beaulieu Bacchus, and Charles Stewart III

SECURING AMERICAN ELECTIONS

How Data-Driven Election Monitoring Can Improve Our Democracy

R. Michael Alvarez
California Institute of Technology

Nicholas Adams-Cohen
Stanford University

Seo-young Silvia Kim
American University

Yimeng Li
California Institute of Technology

CAMBRIDGE
UNIVERSITY PRESS

CAMBRIDGE
UNIVERSITY PRESS

University Printing House, Cambridge CB2 8BS, United Kingdom

One Liberty Plaza, 20th Floor, New York, NY 10006, USA

477 Williamstown Road, Port Melbourne, VIC 3207, Australia

314–321, 3rd Floor, Plot 3, Splendor Forum, Jasola District Centre, New Delhi – 110025, India

79 Anson Road, #06–04/06, Singapore 079906

Cambridge University Press is part of the University of Cambridge.

It furthers the University's mission by disseminating knowledge in the pursuit of education, learning, and research at the highest international levels of excellence.

www.cambridge.org
Information on this title: www.cambridge.org/9781108744928
DOI: 10.1017/9781108887359

First published 2020

A catalogue record for this publication is available from the British Library.

ISBN 978-1-108-74492-8 Paperback
ISSN 2633-0970 (online)
ISSN 2633-0962 (print)

Securing American Elections

How Data-Driven Election Monitoring Can
Improve Our Democracy

Elements in Campaigns and Elections

DOI: 10.1017/9781108887359
First published online: November 2020

R. Michael Alvarez
California Institute of Technology

Nicholas Adams-Cohen
Stanford University

Seo-young Silvia Kim
American University

Yimeng Li
California Institute of Technology

Author for correspondence: R. Michael Alvarez,
rmichaelalvarez@gmail.com

Abstract: The integrity of democratic elections, both in the United States and abroad, is an important problem. In this Element, we present a data-driven approach that evaluates the performance of the administration of a democratic election, before, during, and after Election Day. We show that this data-driven method can help to improve confidence in the integrity of American elections.

Keywords: election security, election audits, election fraud, voter registration, social media, survey methodology, voter confidence

ISBNs: 9781108744928 (PB), 9781108887359 (OC)
ISSNs: 2633-0970 (online), 2633-0962 (print)

Contents

Preface

Election Integrity

The integrity of democratic elections, both in the United States and abroad, is an important problem. From a normative or philosophical perspective, it is difficult to dispute that democratic elections *should* be conducted freely, fairly, and with a high degree of integrity, so that citizens and stakeholders agree that the regime put into power by a democratic election has legitimacy. Election integrity is the foundation for a strong, resilient, and well-functioning representative democracy.

However, how do citizens, candidates, and stakeholders know that an election has been conducted with integrity? How do they know that an election has been conducted freely and fairly, so that they are confident that the ballots have been correctly counted, and that the reported results reflect a truly fair process, one that is free from fraud or administrative error?

These are the difficult questions that we consider in this manuscript. Here we lay out a comprehensive quantitative methodology that evaluates the performance of the administration of a democratic election, before, during, and after Election Day. We focus on quantitative approaches to election evaluation, and we show that a data-driven evaluation provides a variety of important and useful metrics for determining the integrity of an election. We also show how these metrics can be presented so that they can be used by election officials, candidates, the media, citizens, and stakeholders. By building tools and methods that can transparently and quickly provide these evaluative metrics to the public, we can raise awareness of the conduct of election administration, dispel rumors and innuendo, and in the end help to increase the confidence of citizens that an election was conducted with integrity.

In this Element we apply these approaches to document the integrity of American elections. Specifically, we present results from a unique series of studies conducted during the 2018 US midterm elections, in Orange County, California. In the next section, we discuss these studies in more detail, and explain why we focus specifically on the 2018 elections in Orange County. Overall, our goal in working with the Orange County Registrar of Voters

(OCROV) was to understand from the Registrar's perspective what types of evaluative metrics would be useful to them, and to determine what types of analyses of the performance of their election technology and procedures were feasible. As we report in the sections below, we learned a great deal throughout this project. We discovered in detail how elections work in Orange County and in California, developed best practices in syncing our data requests with the OCROV's workflow, and determined which types of methodologies can quickly assess the performance of election technologies and procedures – along with lessons on what did not work as well.

Most importantly, in the highly competitive 2018 midterm elections, our evidence confirms that the election process in Orange County was conducted with integrity. A number of the most competitive US House of Representatives elections in 2018 were in Orange County, and our data-driven approach documents a small number of minor issues in these elections. Placing these minor issues into the larger context of the administration of one of the largest and most diverse election jurisdictions in the United States, we show that few voters experienced problems casting their ballots and that there is a high degree of confidence among voters about the integrity of the election. We thus offer strong evidence confirming the integrity of the administration of this election in 2018 in Orange County. All of these lessons are discussed in the sections of this Element.

1 Trustworthy Elections

1.1 Introduction

In his classic study of electoral politics in the American South, V. O. Key, Jr. wrote: "If a democratic regime is to work successfully it must be generally agreed that contestants for power will not shoot each other and that ballots will be counted as cast" (Key, 1984, p. 443). That was true back in 1949, when Key wrote *Southern Politics*, and it is certainly true today. For a representative democracy to function well, it needs to have a reliable process for administering elections, that process should be free and fair, and all concerned should be convinced of the integrity of the administration of elections. That is, stakeholders, candidates, and voters should all have a high degree of confidence that each and every election is conducted with great integrity – as Key said, "that all ballots will be counted as cast."

Consider this question from the perspective of a registered voter who lives in Costa Mesa, California. Costa Mesa is a community in Orange County, tucked between the beautiful coastal town of Newport Beach (and the Pacific Ocean), and the larger inland cities of Irvine, Santa Ana, and Anaheim. In the 2018 general election in Costa Mesa, there was a hotly contested election for the 48th Congressional seat. This Congressional seat had been held for three decades by a conservative Republican, Dana Rohrabacher. As a Congressman, Rohrabacher supported conservative causes his entire career, getting a score of 94 of 100 by the American Conservative Union (ACU) in 2017, and controversially flaunted his close connections to Russia. In the general election, the incumbent Rohrabacher faced Democrat Harley Rouda, who received financial support from Democrats across the nation in his bid to flip this Republican seat in Orange County.

On election night, it was clear that the race between Rohrabacher and Rouda would be very close: in the first tally reported by the OCROV, Rohrabacher had a slim lead, with 52,451 votes to Rouda's 52,370. As additional ballots were counted on election night, the lead bounced back and forth between the two candidates; by the time the Registrar released the first tally report early in the morning after the election, Rouda had a slight lead of just over 2,200 votes. In the days and weeks following the election, Rouda's lead steadily grew. In the final official results,[1] Rouda had accumulated 157,837 votes, to Rohrabacher's 136,899 – an impressive win by a challenger over a long-time incumbent.

---

[1] Neal Kelley, Orange County Registrar of Voters, *Orange County 2018 General Election, November 6, 2018 Official Results for Election*, www.ocvote.com/fileadmin/live/gen2018/results.htm, last retrieved March 15, 2020.

But our hypothetical voter, who does not know much about election administration, might wonder exactly what went on. Why did such a close election become a strong win for Rouda? Why did the ballots counted days and days after the election favor the Democratic candidate so heavily? Was this a fair process, and were all of the ballots counted as cast? Did Rouda win, fair and square?

Students of election administration may recognize this phenomenon: typically, the first set of ballots counted right away on election night are the absentee by-mail ballots that have been received by the election officials in the days before the election, with those by-mail ballots often coming from Republican-leaning voters in California. Election Day voters, and also provisional voters, often tend to be more Democratic in their preferences, so ballots that get counted in the days and weeks following an election will frequently skew Democratic. There is nothing nefarious about this – but these details are not obvious to most voters.

So how can we help convince this concerned voter in Costa Mesa that the election was conducted fairly, and that the process had a high degree of integrity from start to finish?

Measuring and confirming the integrity of elections is precisely what this Element is about. How can a team of data and political scientists monitor a major and important federal election like the one held in 2018 in Orange County, and produce analytical materials that can be made available to the public in near real-time during an election? How can we quickly produce studies covering all aspects of an election's conduct, and package these analyses for an interested public to read in order to determine whether to trust an election's reported result?

These were the goals of an innovative project in Orange County that our team launched in 2018, and we report the results of this project in this Element. In the sections that follow we will present in detail the types of studies we undertook in Orange County, what we found, and from there outline best practices for future projects like these. To jump to the conclusion, we find that the election was conducted with a high degree of integrity – our data and analyses show that Rouda won the election, and that we can be very confident in the outcome of this and the rest of the elections on the 2018 Orange County ballot.

1.2 Performance Auditing of Elections

In many American states, election officials routinely do some type of post-election auditing – procedures that seek to confirm that the methods and technologies used to tabulate votes operated as expected and that the tabulation process led to reproducible results. These routine postelection ballot audits have been defined by the National Council of State Legislatures (NCSL):[2]

While the phrase "post-election audits" can be used to mean a variety of election validation efforts, as a term of art it refers to checking paper ballots or records against the results produced by the voting system to ensure accuracy. 34 states + DC currently have a post-election audit as defined here. Paper records used in an audit may include voter-marked paper ballots, voter-verified paper audit trails produced by direct-recording electronic voting machines (DREs) or paper ballot records produced by ballot-marking devices. Typically only a sample of the paper records are examined, so in effect a post-election audit is a partial recount of results to verify that the voting system is accurately recording and counting votes.

Postelection ballot audits are powerful evaluative methodologies. By comparing an independent tabulation of the ballots cast in an election, postelection ballot audits can help confirm that the technologies and procedures used for ballot tabulation worked as expected, and if conducted in a public and transparent manner, can help buttress public confidence in the integrity of the ballot tabulation process (Alvarez et al., 2012). There are many different types of postelection ballot audits. The NCSL study shows that the most prevalent type is the "traditional" fixed-percentage audit: a set percentage of ballots cast or voting precincts are selected, and either the ballots selected or the ballots from the sampled precincts are included in the auditing tabulation. Another type is the so-called "risk-limiting" audit (RLA) (Stark, 2009), currently used in a limited (but growing) number of election jurisdictions in the United States. The RLA samples ballots for the postelection audit based on the reported election outcome: the closer the election contest, the greater the number of ballots that will be included in the audit – this helps the RLA confirm the outcome of very close election contests (a property that traditional fixed-percentage audits do not have).

However, as we will discuss in detail in Section 4, all postelection ballot audits are limited to confirming the initial tabulation of ballots. In other words, they are useful for confirming that the initial tabulation was correct, or for confirming that the procedures and technologies used for the initial ballot tabulation worked as expected. Thus, postelection ballot audits are an important tool for confirming the integrity of aspects of an election's administration, but

---

[2] NCSL, *Post-Election Audits*, www.ncsl.org/research/elections-and-campaigns/post-election-audits635926066.aspx, last retrieved March 15, 2020.

they do not help us understand the integrity of the voter registration data, specific problems that voters or poll workers had on Election Day, and whether there were anomalies or problems with the conduct of a jurisdiction's election.

Thus, instead of focusing solely on postelection ballot auditing, in this Element we argue that we should take a broader perspective, and try to evaluate the performance of the complete administration and conduct of an election. This type of holistic and ecological auditing seeks to examine the performance of an election process from end to end, so that a skeptical voter (like our hypothetical voter in Costa Mesa) can have confidence that all aspects of an election, from the registration of voters well before ballots are cast, to the vote-by-mail process, to the postelection tabulation of all ballots, are performing as expected. Our general approach for evaluating the integrity of an election is performance auditing of elections, which builds off of recent work on comprehensive audits of elections, and audits of components of the election process other than ballot tabulation (Alvarez, Atkeson, & Hall, 2012a, 2012b; Selker, 2005). In the remaining sections of this Element, we will present different methodologies and tools (including postelection ballot auditing) that can help us evaluate an election from a holistic and ecological perspective, to gain a broader vision of the integrity of an election from start to finish.

1.3   The 2018 Orange County Project

In the 2018 election cycle, we proposed an ambitious project to examine the utility of different types of quantitative election forensics during a major federal election, in a large election jurisdiction, that would be useful to both the public and to election administrators. For this comprehensive study, we were lucky to be able to work closely with the Orange County Registrar of Voters (OCROV), Neal Kelley, and his team.

We choose to focus on Orange County for a variety of reasons. Orange County is a large and diverse area of Southern California. Located south of Los Angeles and north of San Diego, Orange County is home to a wide array of different businesses, colleges, and universities, and of course, Disneyland. The county currently has a total population of almost 3.2 million residents, and in the 2016 presidential election, Orange County had just over 2 million voting-eligible citizens, with 1.5 million registered voters.[3] In that same election, 1.2 million of those registered voters participated (80.71% of registered

---

[3] Data from the California Secretary of State, http://elections.cdn.sos.ca.gov/sov/2016-general/sov/02-voter-reg-stats-by-county.pdf.

voters).[4] Orange County's population is also quite diverse, as the US Census Bureau's most recent estimates show that 72% of the county's population is White, 21% Asian, 2% Black, and 3.5% two or more races. The Census Bureau's recent data estimates that 34% of the Orange County's population is Hispanic or Latino.[5] Thus, one reason we focus on Orange County for this study is that it is one of the largest and most diverse election jurisdictions in the United States.

Secondly, Orange County is widely viewed as innovative in the administration of elections. The County's Registrar of Voters, Neal Kelley, participates widely in state and national professional organizations, and has been recognized for his innovative administrative practices. Under his administration, Orange County has developed many administrative processes and tools that are viewed as best practices for election administration, for example, building transparency by webcasting in real-time virtually all aspects of the process of administering an election, or more recently, pilot testing risk-limiting audits.

Because of these factors, in 2018 we established a unique collaboration between researchers from the California Institute of Technology and OCROV. The collaboration, which continues today, focuses on developing applications and analytical tools for documenting the integrity of the county's elections (primary and general), with the use of quantitative and qualitative methodologies. One of the important components of this project is the development of the quantitative methodologies that we report on in this Element – methods for quickly analyzing daily snapshots of Orange County's voter registry, in order to efficiently and effectively audit the voter registration database. As part of this component of our collaboration, OCROV agreed to provide *daily* snapshots of their entire voter list, excluding only a small set of fields that contain highly personal and sensitive information (in particular, the voter's California driver's license or identification number, and their Social Security Number). As far as we are aware, this is the first time that a county election jurisdiction in the United States has provided daily voter-file snapshots, with an extensive array of information about each registered voter, over a long period of time, to academic researchers.[6]

---

[4] Data from the California Secretary of State, http://elections.cdn.sos.ca.gov/sov/ 2016-general/sov/03-voter-participation-stats-by-county.pdf.

[5] These figures are from the Census Bureau's July 1, 2017 population estimates, www.census .gov/quickfacts/fact/table/orangecountycalifornia/PST045217.

[6] Scholars of election administration know that certain states make some of their voter registration data available, either by mail (e.g., Florida), or online (e.g., North Carolina or Ohio). While our techniques could be used on data from those jurisdictions, the data we have is more granular (available daily) and has a very extensive set of features for each voter, allowing deeper analyses of record change and of potential duplicates.

1.4   Roadmap

In the sections that follow, we present each of the quantitative methodologies that we have developed and used in our election performance auditing research. Our Element is structured in two parts. The first part presents methodologies that seek to obtain direct evaluative data from participants and observers in elections: social media monitoring of election reports and discussion (Section 2), and surveys of voters and poll workers (Section 3). In the second part of the Element, we turn to statistical forensic methods for evaluating the performance and integrity of an election, using postelection ballot audits and forensic studies of turnout and voting statistics (Section 4), as well as the statistical analysis of voter registration data (Section 5).

We begin in Section 2 with our work that uses social media monitoring, specifically monitoring Twitter, to collect data on election experiences, and concerns about elections, at large scale and in real-time. In this section, we present a number of results that demonstrate the potential utility of social media monitoring for studying election integrity; we also discuss many of the current challenges raised by the collection and analysis of social media data for election monitoring.

Section 3 turns to ways to best measure voter and poll worker experiences. In this section, we focus on directly measuring these experiences using micro-level surveys. Over the past decade, a number of research groups have developed some relatively standard ways to measure voter experience and confidence, and we use many of those measurement approaches in our Orange County work. In this section, we discuss the pros and cons of direct measurement of a voter's experience with online surveys, and we also present some data from poll worker surveys collected by the OCROV.

Moving to Section 4, there we shift the discussion to the use of postelection ballot audits, and other statistical anomaly detection methodologies, that can be used to assess the integrity of components of the electoral process. Postelection ballot audits are used in many states, some using auditing approaches that seek to confirm that the election technology and procedures for balloting worked as expected, while others try to assess whether the election outcome was correct. In 2018, Orange County implemented both types of postelection ballot audit, so we discuss what we can learn from this methodology in the first part of this section. Then we turn to the topic of independent third-party forensic techniques, focusing on the analysis of precinct-level turnout and vote share data, using graphical methods. We present some of the results from the use of these forensic tools in Orange County, and discuss their strengths and weaknesses.

In Section 5, we turn to the important question of monitoring one of the major components of election administration in the United States: evaluating the integrity, accuracy, and security of voter registration databases. In this section, we present a methodology that we have developed to audit and monitor large voter registration databases, a methodology that we have used in Orange County since early 2018 and are now beginning to implement in other counties and states. This section outlines the approach we take to monitoring voter registration databases, shows the information we can obtain using our method, and discusses what the future may hold for quantitative methods that can audit voter registration data.

In the final section, we bring these various methods together to examine, in a holistic and ecological way, what inferences and conclusions we can draw from the data and analysis about the integrity of the 2018 elections in Orange County. We also discuss in this final section some important lessons we have learned in our 2018 research, and some next steps in the development of methods for assessing the integrity and security of American elections.

Finally, our code and data are all publicly available and hosted on GitHub (`https://github.com/monitoringtheelection`). Our project website will also continue to be the host for updates and public reporting about our election integrity projects (`https://monitoringtheelection.us/`).

2 Social Media Monitoring

2.1 Why Monitor Social Media?

The advent of social media has granted voters access to a modern "political forum," a place to discuss the voting process with others in real-time during an election. By tracking voter discussions of elections on social media as they occur, we can begin to observe, highlight, and address specific problems as they arise in the electoral process.

In this way, tracking citizen-provided descriptions of problems and concerns with the voting process is a potential replacement for in-person election monitoring, which many consider the current "gold standard" for detecting election problems. In-person election monitoring, where trained and experienced poll watchers physically observe the election process on-site, allows researchers to gain a highly detailed, qualitative sense of exactly where and when problems in the voting process occur. However, this methodology requires a large investment of time and resources; even with a trained team of poll watchers, only a minuscule fraction of polling places can realistically be observed in a given election. This limited coverage makes in-person election monitoring unfeasible if the goal is to detect problems in a large election jurisdiction, especially when trying to detect low-incidence problems.

Analyzing social media data, on the other hand, can provide wide and detailed coverage across the United States, in specific states, and perhaps in counties. In addition to being far less costly than in-person monitoring, social media data might detect election problems at the scale of a large federal election, an important distinction to previous qualitative efforts. This is true even for low-incidence and geographically concentrated election issues, as discussed later in this section.

Thus, in our effort to develop a well-rounded, ecological approach to monitoring and securing elections, our team created and implemented a social media election monitor during the 2018 midterm elections. Building on previous work analyzing Twitter discussions during electoral cycles (e.g. Adams-Cohen et al., 2017, Lin et al., 2013, McKinney, Houston, & Hawthorne, 2013), we developed a series of scripts and algorithms to collect and store a large volume of social media data. We then analyzed the overall trends in conversations about the 2018 voting process in the days before and after Election Day.

While we collected several months of data, we focus most of this section on our analysis of data collected on November 6, 2018, the date of the midterm election. We first analyze conversations during this 24-hour period to detect problems with the election at the national scale, before using location inference techniques to monitor voting problems at a state and local level. As in the rest of this Element, we focus our local analysis on the Orange County elections.

Even though our approach had some limitations, which we discuss in the conclusion of this section, our work provides a strong foundation for future methods that leverage social media data to better understand and address issues with the electoral process.

2.2   Our Methodology

Our team developed and implemented a methodology to track discussions concerning elections and the voting process by collecting and analyzing Twitter data. With an average of 326 million daily active users[7] and emphasis on sharing immediate reactions to events, Twitter is a rich potential source of information about elections and voting.[8]

---

[7] According to the Q3 2018 Twitter investor statement. See https://investor.twitterinc .com/files/doc_news/archive/4ad1fd92-0dea-4c13-9a71-8674acf154cc.pdf.

[8] See Steinert-Threkeld (2018) for a primer on the best practices in using social media data in the social sciences.

Political scientists use social media datasets to study various aspects of the electoral process, including the way politicians use social media in their political campaigns (Golbeck, Grimes, & Rogers, 2010; Graham, Jackson, & Broersma, 2016; Theocharis, Barberá, Fazekas, Popa, & Parnet, 2016), how the public discusses presidential debates and other major campaign events (Lin et al., 2013; McKinney et al., 2013; Murthy, 2015), and what Twitter networks reveal about political polarization (Barberá, 2015; Conover et al., 2011).

Given Twitter's emphasis on sharing immediate reactions to trending events, many researchers have leveraged the platform as a way to gauge and measure public opinion (Beauchamp, 2017; O'Connor, Balasubramanyan, & Routledge, 2010; Sajuria & Fabrega, 2016). A large body of this work specifically tracks Twitter conversations of politicians and political parties, analyzing these conversations in order to forecast election results (Burnap, Gibson, Sloan, Southern, & Williams, 2016; Ceron, Curini, & Iacus, 2015; Murthy, 2015).

We follow this literature by first collecting Twitter data during a campaign to make inferences about the election process. However, instead of attempting to forecast election results, we turn our attention to measuring the integrity of the election. That is, instead of forecasting the electoral success of specific politicians or political parties, we collect messages in which users describe the voting process, in an attempt to locate potential issues with federal, state, and local elections.

Our collection of Twitter data roughly consists of the following steps:[9]

1. Defining a set of keywords broadly associated with common electoral and voting issues.
2. Setting up a series of Python scripts that interact with the Twitter Streaming API, granting access in real-time to tweets that contain one or more of our track words.
3. Storing each message, including the associated metadata and user information, in a MySQL database.
4. Analyzing the text and metadata of these messages over the election period.

Our team designed this process and implemented early versions in the 2014 election cycle, and we have been working to refine and improve the process in each successive election cycle (Adams-Cohen et al., 2017).

For the 2018 midterm election, we focused on five broad topics: "Election Day voting," "election fraud," "remote voting," "polling places," and "voter identification." Table 1 displays the keywords we monitored for each category.

---

[9] This methodology was initially developed in Adams-Cohen et al. (2017), which contains additional technical details on each specific step in our process.

Table 1 Tracked keywords

Category	Keywords
Election Day Voting	provisional ballot, voting machine, ballot
Voter Fraud	election fraud, election manipulation, illegal voters, illegal votes, noncitizen voting, noncitizen votes, illegal voting, illegal vote, illegal ballot, illegal ballots, dirty voter rolls, vote illegally, voting illegally, voter intimidation, voter suppression, rigged election, vote rigging, voter fraud, voting fraud, ballot destruction, vote flipping, flipped votes, voter coercion, ballot stuffing, ballot box stuffing, vote buying, voting machine tampering, rigged voting machines, voter impersonation, election integrity, election rigging, duplicate voting, duplicate vote, ineligible voting, ineligible vote, dead voters
Remote Voting	absentee ballot, mail ballot, vote by mail, voting by mail, early voting
Voter ID	voter identification, voting identification, voter id
Polling Places	polling place line, precinct line, pollworker, poll worker

While clearly not an exhaustive set of terms related to each category, we leveraged domain expertise to choose a set of terms broad enough to collect the majority of conversations concerning an election topic but narrow enough to stay within a particular issue domain.[10] We solicited input from a number of election administration experts in selecting these keywords.

For each message we collect, we also obtain a rich set of metadata associated with a tweet, including information about the user sending the message. One particularly useful piece of information contained in a tweet's metadata is the user's location. By detecting the origin of a message, it is possible to pinpoint specific states or municipalities experiencing an abnormally large volume of

---

[10] A risk in following a static list of keywords is missing potentially important words and phrases that may develop dynamically during the data collection period (King, Lam, & Roberts, 2017). As we iterate and develop our social media monitor for future elections, we hope to introduce dynamically evolving keywords along the lines of Liu et al. (2019).

conversations about election issues. Detecting the location of social media messages is a rich and developing subfield in the computer science literature (e.g. Hecht et al., 2011, Ikawa, Enoki, & Tatsubori, 2012, Li & Sun, 2014, McGee, Caverlee, & Cheng, 2013). Our group uses two methods to determine the origin of users: embedded geocodes and user-supplied descriptions of locations.

If a user elects to "geotag" their tweet, important geographic information is embedded in the message, including the user's precise longitude and latitude. This represents the "gold standard" for determining which city and state a user is in when they send a tweet. Unfortunately, only around 1% of all tweets are geotagged (Kumar, Morstatter, & Liu, 2015, p. 32), making it difficult to generate a large sample of geo-identified tweets.

Therefore, our team exploits an additional feature of a tweet to determine the location of a Twitter user: the "location" field in a Twitter user's profile. This optionally provided piece of information is less accurate than a geotagged message, given a user can choose to leave this field blank when they set up their Twitter account, fail to update their profile after a move, or provide an inaccurate description of their location (Hecht et al., 2011). Furthermore, given users have complete freedom in describing their location, there is no infallible method to determine the referenced location. As an example, a user from Los Angeles might fill their location field with either "Los Angeles," "LA," or "The City of Angels." Though each of these phrases may refer to the same city, it appears as three unique character strings when sorting through the location field.

To circumvent this problem, our group relied on a large series of regular expressions (sequences of characters that describe specific search patterns) to filter and sort the location data. We sort through all major variations of a state's name, as well as each of the major cities in a state. While not every user provides accurate location data and our regular expressions cannot capture every variation of state and city names, the major advantage of relying on the location field is the much larger number of users who elect to provide some written description of their location compared to users who geotag their messages. These two processes allow us to get a sample of Twitter users from Orange County, and in the last section of this section we focus our analysis on this subgroup to determine whether there seem to be particular concerns about election administration in Orange County.

Beyond difficulties determining the location of users, a possible concern with analyzing Twitter data is the social media platform's potential ability to spread misinformation. One of the primary ways this false information is spread is through "bot" accounts: automated software that sends tweets with the intent to deceive voters (Ferrara, 2017). While a large number of bot accounts could skew the results of our monitor, work analyzing political communication on Twitter finds that less than 15% of users are likely bots (Adams-Cohen et al., 2017; Bessi & Ferrara, 2016; Ferrara, 2017). The number of likely bots drops dramatically when focusing on a subpopulation of users providing some form of location information (Bessi & Ferrara, 2016; Ferrara, 2017), with Howard et al.'s 2017 recent study of the 2016 election in Michigan finding for a "state-specific sub-sample ... only 2% of the platforms used to send Twitter traffic were known sources of bots" (p. 2). Based on these previous analyses, and as a result of focusing much of our analysis on accounts with location data, we conclude there is little evidence that bots produce a large enough number of tweets in our database to heavily skew our results.[11]

2.3   Monitoring the 2018 Election

We ran our social media election monitor continuously from August 5, 2018 to December 12, 2018. In this time, we collected and stored nearly 29 million tweets from over 3.6 million unique users.

To host our social media monitor, we set up a web portal at `https://monitoringtheelection.us`. On this website, we displayed daily snapshots of our social media data stream, including the hourly frequencies of each tracked topic in a 24-hour period, as well as a pie chart to visualize the overall proportion of tweets corresponding to each issue topic. Figure 1 displays an image of our web portal.[12] Our intention with the web portal was to provide a snapshot of the most important issues concerning the election process each day. Of particular interest was the proportion of tweets concerning voter fraud, which highlighted concerns about the electoral process on a given day.

To observe the overall trends in conversations during the entire election cycle, we present the daily number of messages of each tracked topic over the entire collection period in Figure 2. The trends visualized in Figure 2 help validate the merit of our approach; conversations about particular topics rise and fall when expected based on the election cycle. The number one topic by volume was Election Day voting. As expected, tweets concerning this topic slowly rise over time, with a large spike on Election Day, November 6.

Tweets about election fraud were the second most popular category observed in our monitor. Unlike the Election Day voting category, there were a few

---

[11] Even when controlling for "bot" accounts, human Twitter users can still potentially spread rumors and misinformation through a social media network. While there is some work developing tools that use machine learning methods to automatically detect and flag rumors in social media data (see Vosoughi 2015 for an example), we did not implement these nascent methodologies for the current project. However, we plan on adopting these methods as an additional robustness check in future iterations of this work.

[12] See `https://github.com/monitoringtheelection` for the code we developed to run the social media monitor.

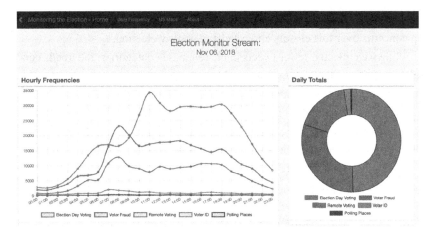

Figure 1 Monitoring The Election website

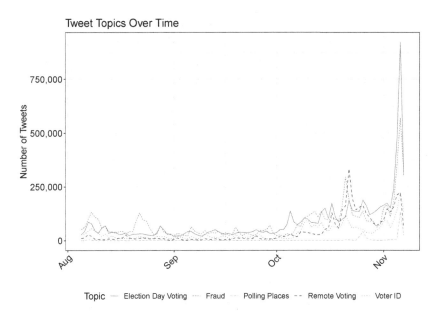

Figure 2 Tracking election topics on Twitter

prominent spikes about fraud at different moments in the election cycle. The first initial spike in early August centers around the time of Ohio's 12th Congressional District special election (August 7, 2018), a contest that ended up being too close to call. In the weeks following the election, 8,400 absentee and provisional ballots were counted (Epstein, 2018). On August 24, 2018, the election was called in favor of Republican Troy Balderson, the day we observe a second spike in August fraud-related tweets. Our monitor was thus able to pick up concerns over this closely contested and narrow election.

While we collected fewer tweets in the remaining categories, the trends correlate strongly with electoral events. Conversations about remote voting spike earlier than conversations about Election Day voting, which makes sense given that citizens vote remotely in the days and weeks leading up to Election Day. Tweets about voter identification seem to follow a similar trend as tweets about Election Day voting, which is intuitive given the topics are highly correlated. Finally, we only find a large number of tweets about polling places on Election Day, the only time users visit polling locations.

2.4   Detecting Problems on Election Day

One major benefit of our social media monitoring method is the ability to analyze issues with voting throughout Election Day. By identifying increased numbers of conversations about specific topics and concerns during an active election, our method can discover problems with the voting process as voting unfolds. While our end goal is to develop an algorithm to automatically detect problems in real-time, our focus in the 2018 election was on collecting and assessing data. With this in mind, in this section we analyze the subset of data concerning election fraud on November 6, 2018, the day of the midterm election.

Over the course of 24 hours, our monitor collected 571,854 total tweets mentioning an election fraud track word by 309,760 unique users.[13] In Figure 3, we visualize how the conversation about election fraud evolved over the course of Election Day.

To get a sense of the content of these tweets, we visualize the most common topics of conversation by creating "word clouds." Word clouds display the most common words across the set of documents, with the size of a word proportional to how often the term appears in the corpus. This allows one to get an overall sense of which terms and phrases are most often mentioned across a set of documents.

In order to create word clouds, we first remove all textual information that does not alter the substance of the message, including punctuation, all forms of capitalization, numbers, hyperlinks, and "stop words," which are common words that do not add to the meaning of a document.[14] Next, we tokenize the text, which splits tweets into individual words and phrases utilizing white

---

[13] Given many users retweet popular messages, these 571,854 total tweets correspond to 107,259 unique messages.

[14] Stop words include tokens such as "the," "of," and "or."

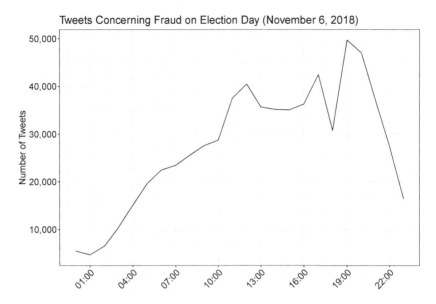

Figure 3 Tracking tweets about fraud on Election Day

space. We first tokenize the corpus into unigrams (single words) but additionally tokenize into bigrams (two-word phrases). Because our data was collected utilizing a series of track words, these words and phrases will, by definition, be among the most common occurring phrases in the dataset. Therefore, for the purposes of creating word clouds, we create one corpus consisting *entirely* of track words and *remove* track words from all remaining corpora.

One unique feature of Twitter data is the ability to use a hashtag (#) to "tag" a tweet with a specific phrase or message. These labels allow users to endow their tweets with an underlying meaning or mark it as belonging to a specific conversation topic. Creating a separate corpus consisting entirely of hashtags is another way we can quickly get a sense of trending conversation.

On tokenizing the set of tweets into unigrams, bigrams, and hashtags, we create word clouds of the most common set of tokens across the election fraud tweets collected on the day of the midterm election.[15]

Figure 4 displays each word cloud based on the four tokenization strategies. We additionally plot the frequency of the top ten most common tokens of each word cloud in Figure 5.

Figure 4a displays our predefined keywords concerning election fraud (see Table 1 for the full list of track words). The two most commonly used phrases

---

[15] The word clouds were produced using the quanteda package (Benoit & Nulty, 2016), which was also used to preprocess and tokenize the text data. We limit the size of a word cloud to display only the top 100 most frequently occurring tokens.

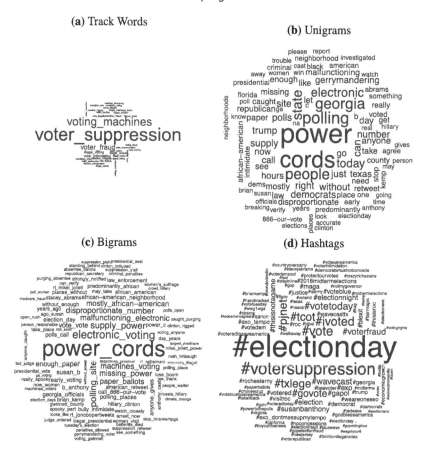

Figure 4 Common words and phrases associated with fraud on Election Day

by far were "voter suppression" and "voting machines." This indicates that one of the most common sets of problems during the 2018 midterm elections involved certain polling places having issues with electronic voting machines. When these machines failed, it led to long lines and frustrated voters, which eventually gave way to concerns about vote suppression.

In Figure 4b, we see that the two most common unigrams were "power" and "cords." This is in reference to the fact that some of the trending stories on Election Day involved polling places where citizens could not cast their vote because of electronic voting machines missing their power cords (Breuninger, 2018). Another commonly occurring phrase is "Georgia," referencing the problems present in several of Georgia's polling places (explored in more detail in Section 3.4.1).

Figure 4c shows the most common bigrams, and again points to issues involving electronic voting machines. In Figure 5c, we see other top-ten

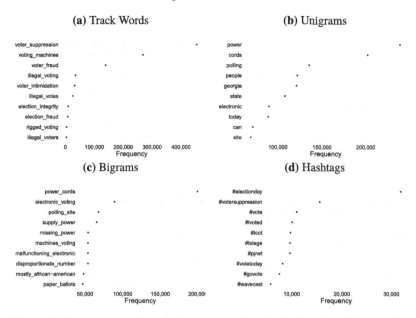

Figure 5 Common words and phrases associated with fraud on Election Day

bigrams include "power cords," "electronic voting," "supply power," "missing power," "machines voting," and "malfunctioning electronic," all phrases that are clearly related to issues concerning electronic voting machines. Other prominent phrases in Figure 4c include the tokens "African American," which points to general concerns with perceived voter suppression and difficulties in voting in certain precincts with high numbers of Black voters.

Moving to Figure 4d, we note the most common hashtag in the word cloud is, perhaps unsurprisingly, #electionday. The next most common phrase we find is #votersuppression. This indicates that, on Election Day itself, a large number of tweets were concerned with potentially depressed turnout. This hashtag was likely contained in many of the messages about malfunctioning electronic voting equipment, as these situations led to long lines at polling places and many frustrated voters being unable to cast their ballot.

Looking at the top ten most common hashtags in Figure 5d, we see more generic hashtags that relate to the voting process, such as #vote, #ivoted, #votetoday, and #govote. Some of the other hashtags are partisan indicators, with #tcot referring to "Top Conservatives on Twitter" and #pjnet referring to "Patriotic Journalist Network," both tags associated with conservative and Republican groups. #wavecast, on the other hand, is a reference to the "Blue Wave," a Democratic movement to take back Congress in the 2018 midterm election. While these hashtags fail to point at specific issues in the election process, the ability to differentiate between liberal and conservative opinions concerning election fraud could prove useful in future iterations of our election monitor.

2.4.1   Fraud Detection at the State Level: Georgia

In Figure 4b, we found that one of the unigrams closely associated with election fraud was "Georgia," demonstrating that a large number of users were tweeting about issues with the elections in this particular state. In order to investigate which states were most frequently referenced in tweets concerning voter fraud, we use a series of regular expressions to count the number of times a specific state was mentioned. By observing which state names are most frequently mentioned, we can determine which elections faced the most allegations of fraud on Election Day.

The results of this analysis are provided in Figure 6. In this map, we use a gradient to highlight the number of times tweets mention each state. Figure 6 immediately reveals the unusually high number of messages mentioning Georgia as compared to other states.

This abnormally large number of messages mentioning Georgia indicates potential issues with that state's midterm election. This did end up being the case, with the 2018 Governor's race in Georgia between Republican Brian Kemp and Democratic challenger Stacey Abrams inundated with complaints about malfunctioning voting machines and voter suppression (Dreyfuss, 2018). Concerns over Georgia's elections eventually led the Abrams campaign to file a lawsuit against the state of Georgia, with Abrams arguing voter suppression was so widespread it had led to an unfair election result (Williams, 2018).

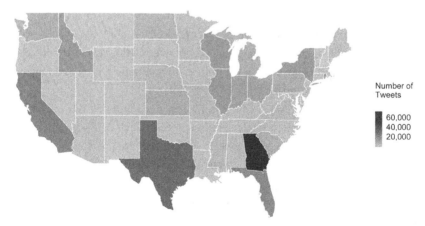

Figure 6 Geographical distribution of tweets about fraud on Election Day

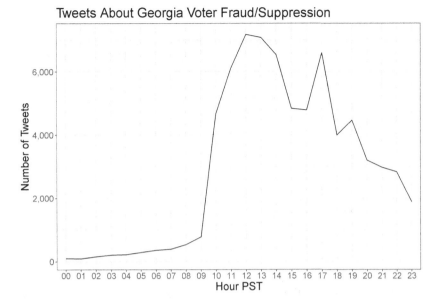

Figure 7 Tweets concerning fraud in Georgia on Election Day

The main benefit of our social media monitor is not simply auditing election problems after they occur, but the possibility of detecting these problems in real-time. While we did not implement real-time issue detection in the 2018 midterms, for future elections we plan on using the temporal nature of Twitter data to detect problems as they unfold. For example, in Figure 7 we plot the number of tweets mentioning fraud in Georgia on Election Day. This figure reveals the large spike in mentions of voting issues in Georgia as early as 12 p.m. PST, before many media groups had widely broadcast any concerns about Georgia's election. By looking for these abnormal spikes in mentions of specific states, we hope to eventually flag issues with the voting process as they occur.

2.4.2   Fraud Detection at the Local Level: Orange County

While social media monitoring is useful in detecting election irregularities at the national or state level, it remains to be seen whether these tools can be helpful in monitoring local elections. In an effort to test how well we can detect local issues, we focus on analyzing tweets sent by users in Orange County.

As described in Section 2.2, we use both geotags and the location field of a user's profile to locate users residing in Orange County. In total, of the roughly 29 million tweets our monitor collected between August 5, 2018 and

Table 2 Proportion of fraud tweets on Election Day

	Number of Tweets	Number of Fraud Tweets	Proportion of Fraud Tweets
All States	1,655,476	571,854	0.345
California	80,714	27,249	0.338
Orange County	4802	1546	0.322
Irvine	464	131	0.282
Anaheim	390	110	0.282
Huntington Beach	233	78	0.335
Newport Beach	202	91	0.450
Santa Ana	141	33	0.234

December 12, 2018, 360,006 messages contained geotags. Of these tweets, 259,680 messages were sent from the United States, 28,216 of these from California, and only 1942 of those from one of the cities in Orange County. Clearly, not enough Twitter users utilize geotags to enable researchers to pull a reasonably sized sample from Orange County to make meaningful inferences.

Luckily, far more users provide information about their location in their user profile. Of the 29 million tweets we collected, 19.5 million came from users who provided some information in their location field, roughly 67 percent of all users. Overall, we determine that about 1.1 million messages were sent from California and 77,000 messages from Orange County over the course of the entire data collection period. While a small subset of the total messages we collected, this sample may be large enough to analyze elections in Orange County. In order to detect voting issues in Orange County on Election Day, we focus on the 4,802 messages that were sent on November 6, 2018 – Election Day itself.

Even with this small sample of messages, we are able to gain insight into which cities in Orange County experienced the most concern about voter fraud by calculating the relative proportion of messages mentioning fraud compared to the other issues we tracked (Election Day voting, voter identification, polling places, and remote voting). That is, for some city l in Orange County, we divide the number of messages we collect about voter fraud by the total number of tweets we collect across each issue category. The higher this quotient, the more concerned users from city l were about voter fraud relative to other aspects of the voting process.

The results of this analysis are found in Table 2. We first note that, across the full set of tweets collected on Election Day (all states), 35% of the messages concerned election fraud. This is very similar to the proportion of California users (34%). While these numbers do not mean anything in themselves, they give us a benchmark to compare to Orange County users. We see that for Orange County, 32% of the total messages involved discussions of voter fraud. This is lower than the state and national averages, which might point to fewer Orange County voters expressing concern about fraud in the election process, although this may also be noise due to a smaller sample size.

Small samples are an even greater concern as we restrict attention to messages from users from specific cities in Orange County. Despite these small samples, we note that Huntington Beach was close to the national average, while Irvine, Anaheim, and Santa Ana had fewer relative messages about voter fraud. The one exception was Newport Beach, with 45% of the total messages focusing on voter fraud. Investigating these messages might point to specific problems with voting in this area.

Even though we present a possible statistic with which to detect voting irregularities at the local level in Table 2, we also note the limitations this method presents. First and foremost, the overall difficulty in determining user locations is compounded when we attempt to restrict attention to the county level. In order to allow for better inferences in local elections, we may need to rely on more advanced methods of determining user locations.

On the other hand, even though small samples impact our ability to make unassailable conclusions about the election in Orange County, it is encouraging to note the relatively small number of messages concerning fraud we detect in the county. With over 1.5 million registered voters in Orange County and what was widely considered a highly contested series of Congressional elections, we believe if there had been a major failure in the election process, our team would have been able to detect these issues in the same way we found problems in the Georgia election.[16] In other words, the relatively low incidence of tweets about voter issues and concerns in Orange County seems to suggest few issues with the election's administration. While we cannot make conclusive statements based on this evidence alone, these findings are consistent with subsequent sections – all evidence suggests the Orange County elections were run with high levels of integrity.

---

[16] To compare, Georgia is a state with 7 million registered voters.

2.5   What Did We Learn?

As voters increasingly discuss elections and the voting process online, social media monitors can serve as important and powerful prognosis tools for officials. As we further develop our ability to detect potential issues with state and local elections and report these problems to officials in real-time, we increase election administrators' ability to solve potential problems with the voting process on Election Day itself. In this section, we outline our unique methodology for gathering, storing, and analyzing social media data.

Looking at the data over the entire election cycle, we note that our method of defining sets of keywords associated with broad categories of voting issues works as intended. Increases in the number of tweets in a specific topic area correlate well with real-world events.

Narrowing our analysis to the data we collected concerning fraud on Election Day, we demonstrate how our approach is capable of detecting problems with the voting process. Our content analysis detected malfunctioning voter machines and voter suppression as the major concerns in the 2018 midterm election. We also reveal Georgia as the state with the most problems with the voting process this election cycle, a finding confirmed by numerous news stories in the postelection news cycle. As we continue to iterate and improve our methodology, we will be able to use the dynamic nature of Twitter data to discover these problems in real-time.

Finally, we demonstrate how to use social media monitoring to detect problems with state and local elections. We successfully leverage geotags and user-provided location information to create a large dataset of users we can identify as living in a specific state. When using our location detection algorithms to generate a subsample of users from Orange County, we did not find a large number of tweets indicating problems in the county on Election Day. Despite small-sample issues precluding us from drawing sweeping and definitive conclusions, our analysis indicates few issues with fraud in the Orange County elections, similar to our findings in subsequent sections. In the future, our group hopes to use additional location inference methods developed in the machine-learning literature to increase the number of users we can determine live in Orange County.

In summary, our group developed and tested a unique methodology to exploit social media data as a means of monitoring elections. We demonstrate how our monitor can successfully detect problems at a national and state scale, and believe with future iterations, these algorithms can pinpoint problems at a county or precinct level.

As we continue to develop our methodology, we will focus on four areas of improvement. First and foremost, we plan to implement methods to flag rumors and misinformation. While we believe "bot" accounts do not radically skew our results, human accounts still have the potential to amplify and spread rumors. While such information is useful in that it helps us to analyze the degree of *perceived* irregularities with the voting process, in order to determine which issues represent legitimate causes for concern during an election we plan on implementing methodologies to automatically detect and flag rumors in social media data (Vosoughi, 2015). Second, future iterations of our methodology will incorporate a more dynamic keyword-tracking monitor, whereby the specific terms we follow will change during the election cycle, as developed in Liu et al. (2019). Third, we will use more advanced and sophisticated geographic location inference techniques, which will grant us more detailed geospatial data and improve our ability to detect problems at a local scale. Finally, we will continue to develop our web portal, which will allow us to provide close to real-time visualizations of issues during an election as they occur. We believe these tools will provide greater transparency of the electoral process, and increase the speed and efficiency with which problems with election administration can be detected in future.

3 Voter and Poll Worker Surveys

3.1 What Can Surveys Tell Us?

The free and fair administration of elections is crucial to a democratic system, and voters who participate in the elections are consumers of services provided by election administrators. Understanding how satisfied voters are with these services and how confident they are about the integrity of the election administration is critical to a democracy. Therefore, we want to measure problems that arise for voters during all stages of the voting process and for every manner of casting a ballot, by collecting comprehensive data in order to understand voter confidence in the democratic process.

Surveys are a powerful tool to this end. First, surveying registered voters allows us to potentially discover problems that may have interfered with their ability to cast their votes as intended. In our survey of registered voters, we asked in-person voters if they had encountered any problems when they tried to vote, such as issues with registration, long lines, and malfunctioning voting machines. Our survey instrument was also designed to uncover problems associated with obtaining, completing, and returning mail ballots for by-mail voters. Ensuring the quality of the registration and voting experience is at the core of the election administrator's job. Our survey taps into various stages of the voting process for both in-person and by-mail voters to provide a comprehensive evaluation.

Second, surveys allow us to elicit respondents' attitudes and perceptions which are typically unavailable in observational or administrative data. In our survey, we asked voters who participated in the November 2018 general election about their level of confidence that votes at different administrative levels had been counted as intended. Voter confidence is an important electoral performance measure and speaks to concerns about how to measure the public's perception of problems with election administration and electoral integrity (Atkeson, Alvarez, & Hall, 2015). How confident voters are that their ballots will be counted correctly is a normative issue within a representative democracy, as a lack of confidence threatens the perceived legitimacy of an elected government (Alvarez, Hall, & Llewellyn, 2008). Aggregating the survey responses, we can quantify voter confidence about vote counting in a jurisdiction, which provides a direct measure of the performance of election administrators. Our analysis also sheds light on what can be done to boost voter confidence.

Third, surveying registered voters allows us to measure the level of other concerns that may lead voters to question electoral integrity and the legitimacy of elected officials. Our survey included questions concerning opinions about the prevalence of voter or election fraud and the system's susceptibility to hacking by foreign governments.

Postelection surveys of registered voters serve as an important addition to the other methods of information-gathering in this Element. Monitoring social media (Section 2) facilitates detecting problems in the electoral process in real-time, but limited access to geolocation information for posts and demographic information for the accounts studied may present difficulties in the study of local elections and different demographic groups. Forensic analysis of ballot counts (later presented in Section 4) can help find anomalies in election data, but a fairly conducted election requires more than a correct tabulation of ballots cast. Voter surveys enable us to target voters in a particular jurisdiction and, by utilizing self-reported or verified demographic information, to analyze and compare voter experience and confidence by important demographics such as age, gender, and race.

In addition to surveys on registered voters, we also analyze poll worker surveys conducted by the Registrar's office. Poll workers play an essential role in the administration of elections (Alvarez & Hall, 2006). They are at the front-lines of any election, whether working in an early voting center or in Election

Day polling places. Thus, surveying this population after an election is essential in order to gain a comprehensive understanding of their perceptions of the integrity of the process, and in particular for documenting problems that arise during the course of their activities.

We build upon our knowledge from the survey methodology literature, using established questions from existing large-scale academic surveys on voter confidence and election experiences, as well as input from the Orange County Registrar of Voters (OCROV) in the design of our survey instrument. As academic researchers, we anonymize survey responses and report results based on anonymized data. Therefore, we may elicit more truthful responses than election administrators themselves, providing an unbiased portrait of the election's administration. Unlike most other academic surveys on public opinion and elections, including ones we conducted independently during the election cycle, our registered voter survey is apolitical in nature and focuses heavily on questions pertinent to evaluating Orange County's 2018 elections, thus providing important feedback to the OCROV, to voters, and to other stakeholders in addition to academic scholars.[17]

3.2 Survey Implementation and Methodology

In this section, we discuss how we use survey methods to assess the experiences, confidence, and opinions of registered voters using surveys, and how we conducted and analyzed our survey of Orange County registered voters in November 2018.

When dealing with a very large population, such as all the registered voters in a jurisdiction, the first step is to determine a sample of the overall population to contact. After determining this sample, the selected registered voters are contacted and invited to participate in the survey. There are two issues that arise with respect to any survey conducted in this manner. First, most surveys do not attempt to interview the entire electorate in a jurisdiction, thus the survey is subject to sampling error. Second, it is infeasible to reach all registered voters, and many registered voters included in the sample may not respond to the survey invitation – creating coverage and contact error. These are typical issues for surveys of all types, and survey methodologists have various methods of diagnosing and dealing with these issues.

In our survey, we contacted via email registered voters who we had email addresses for and invited them to participate in our voter experience survey

---

[17] Some past research has indicated that survey topic can influence survey response, so our approach was to design an apolitical survey to maximize survey response from less politically interested registered voters (Groves et al., 2004).

between Thursday, November 8, 2018 and Tuesday, November 13, 2018. From 531,777 invites to registered voters with email addresses, we received 6,952 complete responses.

After collecting the responses, we compared the respondent sample and target population in terms of key demographic and political characteristics, such as age, gender, race/ethnicity, and party affiliation. Oftentimes, the registered voters who voluntarily participate in a survey are not a representative sample of the population of registered voters as a whole. When a statistical analysis of survey responses is conducted without taking into account the nature of voluntary participation, the results only speak to the survey sample at hand and hence may provide an inaccurate portrait of the experiences and opinions of the registered voter population in a jurisdiction. The primary way that researchers deal with the discrepancy between the characteristics of the survey sample and the target population of interest is a procedure known as calibration weighting (Deville & Sarndal, 1992). Calibration weighting aims to ensure the weighted sample matches the target population in terms of an array of prespecified characteristics by imposing minimal up- or down-weighting of individual responses. Intuitively, if permanent absentee voters are overrepresented in the sample, to get estimates representative of registered voters in a jurisdiction as a whole, researchers impose minimal down-weighting so that the weighted sample has the same fraction of permanent absentee voters as the population.

Among respondents who completed our survey, we are able to determine basic demographic information for 6,912 respondents and our analysis will be based on their responses.[18] Figure 8 shows the demographic composition and the distributions of other individual characteristics for our survey respondents and the population of Orange County registered voters before the November 2018 general election.

Registered voters of different ages and genders are well represented in our survey sample. There are slightly more (2.7%) respondents between 30 and 44 years old, fewer (4.4%) respondents from age group 45–64, and fewer (2.0%) female respondents, compared to the population of registered voters. Our survey sample exhibits the most imbalances in race/ethnicity and party registration. More white voters and fewer Hispanic or Latino and Asian American voters participated in the survey (by 8.7%, 6.1%, and 6.0% respectively). Meanwhile, while 34.7% of voters were registered with the Republican Party in Orange County, only 24.0% of those who completed our survey are Republican

---

[18] Demographic information such as age, gender, and race/ethnicity is important for determining the appropriate survey weights for the analysis of our survey.

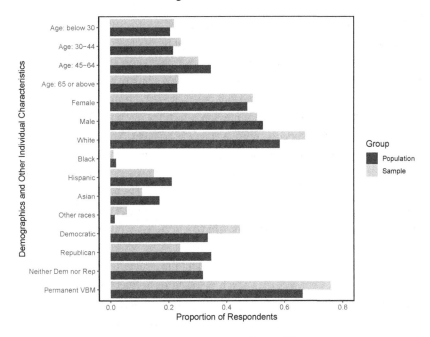

Figure 8 Respondent composition of the survey

voters. On the other hand, 44.6% of respondents are Democratic voters, compared to 33.5% in the population. The disparities in terms of race/ethnicity and party registration in our survey sample are expected given our knowledge about survey participation in general, and consistent with other surveys with voluntary participation. Finally, 66.2% of registered voters in Orange County are permanent vote-by-mail voters, whereas the percentage is 75.8% in our sample; the distribution of cities of residence for our sample tracks the population well.

In short, our sample differs from the target population in terms of individual characteristics such as race/ethnicity, party affiliation, and permanent absentee voter status. To make our analysis representative of Orange County-registered voters, we use a calibration weighting procedure, as discussed earlier. Specifically, we use *raking*, and our raking algorithm uses information on age, gender, race/ethnicity, party registration, permanent absentee ballot status, and city of residence to produce weights that we use in our statistical analyses to produce more representative results. We provide further details about our raking procedure in Appendix A1.

One important consideration for designing a useful survey is the format of survey questions. While closed-ended questions are more amenable to statistical analysis, open-ended responses have traditionally been considered more difficult to analyze (Schuman & Presser, 1996). As a result, the majority of survey analyses today are composed predominantly of closed-ended questions. Despite the complexities of their analysis, we believe open-ended questions have a unique advantage for some issues regarding voter experiences. Election administration is ever-changing, so that issues arising during an election cycle can be very different from those of previous elections. Despite election administrators' continuing efforts to improve voter experiences, a full enumeration of problems beforehand is infeasible. Moreover, advances in text-analytical tools have made the analysis of open-ended survey responses easier and less time-consuming than formerly. Our questionnaire consists of both closed-ended and open-ended questions, where open-ended questions focus on problems with voter registration and issues that may have interfered with voters' ability to cast their vote as intended.

To analyze open-ended questions, we adopt the structural topic model proposed by Roberts et al. (2014), which is based on influential work by Blei, Ng, and Jordan (2003). While we discuss the technical details in Appendix A2, it is useful to think of each survey response as covering one or more topics, with each topic summarized by a few representative words. Intuitively, a survey response may be about two topics: (1) the problem of not receiving mail ballots and (2) the problem of a voter's name not appearing on the roster, with each topic corresponding to words associated with that topic and their frequencies of occurrence. For example, the topic of not receiving mail ballots may be represented by a distribution of words concentrated on "ballots," "receive," "mail," "never," and "arrive." The important outputs from the structural topic model for us are a list of top topics and representative words and exemplar documents for each topic. As we shall see, the structural topic model is a powerful tool for quickly summarizing a large number of open-ended responses and, in our context, highlighting important problems that voters encountered.

We also take several measures of survey quality control to bolster the confidence in the results we draw. At the survey level, after approximately each quarter of the survey, we included an attention filter to gauge whether the recorded responses reflected careful and not haphazard clicks. The attention filters are of two types, known as instructional manipulation checks (Berinsky, Margolis, & Sances, 2014) and instructed response items (Alvarez et al., 2019). We report our results based on the whole sample but also confirm that the results are qualitatively the same if we deal with inattentive responses following different approaches summarized in Alvarez et al. (2019). At the question level, we randomize the order of response options wherever plausible (between the ascending and descending order for ordered options) and randomize between a grid format and a nongrid format for questions on voter confidence at different levels. Such randomizations aim to minimize the effect of option orders and question formats. We pool different option orders and question formats in the analysis with the assurance that our results are largely the same across subsets of respondents receiving each randomization.

3.3 Voter Evaluations

The survey took about 10 to 15 minutes to complete (the median duration was 13 minutes) and included questions on in-person or by-mail voting experience, voter confidence, and perceptions of voter fraud and computer hacking in addition to basic demographic questions. The survey questions were developed to maintain as much comparability as possible with statewide and national voter experience surveys, including other statewide surveys that we had implemented in 2018, as well as surveys like the Survey of the Performance of American Elections and the Cooperative Congressional Election Study.[19]

3.4 In-Person Voting Experiences

For all voters reporting they voted or attempted to vote in the November 2018 general election, our survey included additional questions about their in-person or vote-by-mail voting experiences. These results are given in Figure 9.

Importantly, 97% of voters reported it was easy to find their polling place. After further investigation into the polling places that some voters found difficult to locate, we could not find any locations with more than two respondents who reported difficulty in finding that location, nor was such difficulty associated with the type of building in which the polling place was located. We nonetheless identify six polling places that may need clearer signs.

Similarly, 91% found the polling place management satisfactory. A vast majority of voters either did not see any problems at their polling places or witnessed only minor problems that did not interfere with the voting process. We identify eight polling places where three or more respondents reported seeing minor or major problems that affected the ability of some people to vote, indicating the need for better management in future elections at these locations. Across different types of polling places, respondents reported witnessing better management at locations inside government office buildings and worse management at community and senior centers.

---

[19] For more information about the Survey of the Performance of American Elections, see https://electionlab.mit.edu/research/projects/survey-performance-ame rican-elections/; additional information about the Cooperative Congressional Election Survey can be found at https://cces.gov.harvard.edu/.

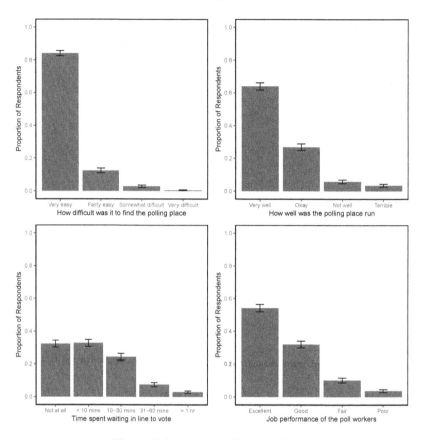

Figure 9 In-person voting experience

Of the surveyed registered voters who voted in person, 86% did not encounter problems with their registration when checking in to vote. This means the vast majority of voters moved on to vote smoothly without registration issues, but it is important to analyze the issues that some voters encountered. For the 14% who reported a problem with their voter registration, we apply the structural topic model to analyze open-ended responses on the problems they encountered. We first follow standard practices to remove punctuation and reduce words to word stems so that variants of a word (e.g., "receive," "received," and "receiving") are identified with their stem (e.g., "receiv").[20] We then fit a ten-topic structural topic model with age, gender, education, race/ethnicity, and party registration as the covariates. Table 3 displays the top five topics for the sake of brevity with the top words associated with them.

---

[20] We used the standard Porter's word-stemming algorithm implemented by R SnowballC library.

Table 3 Top topics concerning problems with registration

Topic 1	ballot, receiv, mail, regist, never, arriv, voter
	receiv, arriv, regist, perman, never, record, ballot
Topic 2	list, name, registr, voter, find, yes, need
	name, registr, yes, roll, gave, list, registrar
Topic 3	ballot, mail, provision, never, absente, said, sent
	provision, ballot, absente, sent, submit, mail, ever
Topic 4	machin, line, one, get, long, worker, wait
	line, get, long, park, hour, lot, machin
Topic 5	vote, didnt, said, show, want, envelop, let
	didnt, let, surrend, vote, show, envelop, believ

To better understand the content of a topic and interpret its meaning, we examine responses that are highly associated with each topic. The top topic concerns voters who did not receive their ballot in the mail. The second most frequent issue that voters reported is that the poll workers had trouble finding their names on the list. Supplementing the results from the structural topic model, a simple word count shows that the keywords "list" and "name" appear in 9.8% and 7.7% of the responses from those who indicated a problem, respectively. Topic 3 regards voters who had to vote provisionally because their registration status indicated that they should have received a vote-by-mail ballot. A typical response stated that the respondent had been told by poll workers that they had signed up as voting by mail according to the record, even though they believed they had not. Among those who indicated a problem, 19.9% of the respondents mentioned the word "provisional." The fourth topic indicates another common problem reported by voters: long lines before voting, either due to machine problems or having only one book at a polling place to verify voter registration. In particular, the keyword "machine" appears in 5.6% of all open-ended responses indicating problems. The last topic again refers to vote-by-mail ballots, but focuses on respondents having had to vote provisionally even after surrendering their vote-by-mail ballots.[21] Overall, among voters who reported having encountered problems, 40.4% mentioned the word "mail." Looking through these responses indicates there were several types of issues involving vote-by-mail ballots, including voters failing to receive their

---

[21] During the Election Day observations our team conducted, it was noted that some voters surrendered their vote-by-mail ballot, so that they could vote in person. In most locations, poll workers followed procedure: they wrote "SURRENDERED" on the back of the vote-by-mail envelope, and placed the vote-by-mail materials in the SURRENDERED/SPOILED ballot envelope located at the official table. Our observers, however, noticed some confusion about handling of the surrendered ballots in a few cases.

mail ballots, believing they never registered as vote-by-mail, and experiencing issues surrendering their ballots at polling places.

We asked voters about their waiting time at polling places, as this has been a problem for some other parts of the country in previous elections. About two-thirds of voters waited in line for less than 10 minutes before they were able to cast their votes, and 10% of them had to wait for more than half an hour. The waiting time is largely attributable to the check-in process for most registered voters (71%), and particularly so for voters who reported having to wait for more than half an hour (76%). The waiting time varies dramatically depending on the time of the day. As one would expect, voters had to wait longer during peak hours, namely before 8 a.m. (poll opening) and after 5 p.m. (poll closing). Among voters who had to wait for more than 30 minutes, 23% arrived at polling places before 8 a.m. and 36% arrived after 5 p.m. The busiest hour is between 5 and 6 p.m., and 29% of respondents who arrived at the poll during this hour reported having to wait for more than half an hour. The waiting time did not vary much by which type of building a polling place was located in.

Finally, few voters (7%) encountered problems with the voting equipment or ballot. Eighty-six percent of the voters rated the poll workers at their polling locations as excellent or good.

3.4.1   By-Mail/Absentee Voting Experiences

For registered voters in our sample who voted by mail or with absentee ballots, more than half (58%) had signed up to receive a mail or absentee ballot automatically in each election. Apart from permanent absentee voters, many reported that voting by mail or as an absentee was more convenient in this election (25%). Other main reasons for voting by mail or as an absentee include being out of town (5%) and work or school schedule (4%).

In total, 95% of voters did not have problems getting their absentee or mail-in ballots. For the 5% who reported problems with getting absentee or mail-in ballots, the main problems were not receiving their mail ballots until they had first called the Registrar of Voters, getting mail ballots too close to the election, receiving mail ballots at previous addresses, and getting mail ballots despite not requesting them. Only 3% had problems marking or completing their ballot that may have interfered with their ability to cast their vote as intended, and almost all (98%) voters found it easy to follow all the instructions necessary to cast their ballot and return it.

3.4.2   Voter Confidence

In the survey, we included a series of questions about whether those who reported to vote in the November 2018 general election were confident that

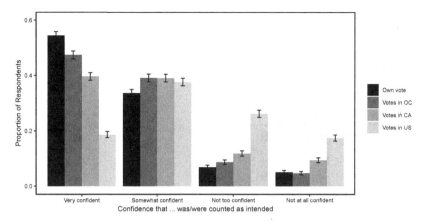

Figure 10 Voter confidence

their own vote had been counted as they intended. We then asked the entire group of surveyed registered voters how confident they were that votes had been correctly counted in Orange County, the State of California, and nationally. Overwhelmingly, we found that those who turned out to vote in Orange County were strongly confident that their vote had been counted as they intended: 88% of the voters in our sample said they were very confident or somewhat confident of this (black bars in Figure 10). The gray bars in the same figure provide similar estimates, but for all surveyed registered voters, regarding their confidence that votes were counted as intended in Orange County. In total, 87% said they were very confident or somewhat confident.

Moving to evaluations of confidence for the state and nation, our Orange County respondents indicated less confidence that votes had been counted as intended. Regarding statewide confidence, 79% said they were very or somewhat confident that votes in California had been counted as intended. And at the national level, 56% of surveyed registered voters indicated confidence in the counting of votes. These results are consistent with academic research arguing that voter confidence is "a local matter" (Atkeson & Saunders, 2007). We investigated factors associated with differences in voter confidence in depth in Alvarez, Cao, and Li (2020). Among other factors, our results indicate that voters who cast mail ballots are less confident about their own votes being counted correctly than in-person voters, and for both types of voters, those who have poor experiences with the voting process are much less likely to report confidence in the election.

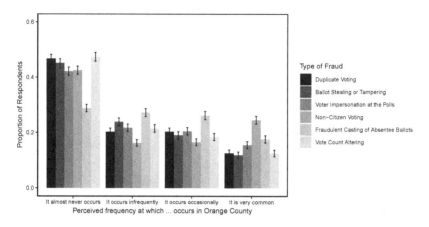

Figure 11 Perception of voter fraud

3.4.3   Perceptions of Voter Fraud and Hacking

We also asked respondents to our survey questions about general perceptions of voter fraud and hacking of election technology. The first set of questions, on perceptions of voter fraud, are given in Figure 11. These questions were presented to survey respondents in a set, in an attempt to ascertain their opinions about how frequently various forms of election fraud might occur in Orange County.

We asked about six types of election fraud: people voting more than once in an election, people stealing or tampering with ballots that have been cast, people pretending to be someone else when going to vote, people voting who are not US citizens, people voting with an absentee ballot intended for another person, and officials changing the reported vote count in a way that is not a true reflection of the ballots that were actually counted.

In general, Orange County-registered voters indicated they believed most potential forms of election fraud, including people voting more than once in an election, people stealing or tampering with voted ballots, voter impersonation, and officials not reporting the vote count correctly, occur infrequently or not at all in Orange County.

We see deviations from this general tendency in two areas: people voting who are not US citizens (26% of our respondents indicated that this was "very common"), and people voting an absentee ballot intended for another person (28% of our respondents indicated that this occurred "occasionally"). There is no indication that these issues actually arise in Orange County; however, we will examine these data in more detail in the future to better understand what might be driving these responses to these two questions.

Finally, we asked two questions about the potential for hacking of election administration in 2018, both locally and nationally. Here we see a pattern similar to that for voter confidence: a majority of Orange County – registered voters responded that they did not believe computer hacking was a problem in Orange County in 2018 (54%). However, there appears to be more concern among Orange County – registered voters regarding computer hacking nationally in 2018: 27% believed it was a major problem, while 46% said it was a minor problem.

3.5　Poll Worker Evaluations

Following both the June primary election and the November general election, the Registrar's office asked poll workers to assess the various components of their experience, including any issues encountered at their polling place. We focus on the general election survey in this section. Given the essential role of poll workers in the administration of elections, data collected from the poll worker survey are informative about the quality and effectiveness of election administrators' services as well as methods of improving election operations. Among 5,215 poll workers who served on Election Day, 1,614 opted to fill out the survey, yielding a response rate of 31%. A majority of respondents had served as poll workers for 3 years or less, with community services, patriotism, and personal interest or curiosity being the top three motivations.

Poll workers were asked about their overall experience serving in the election, their rating of the overall quality of Registrar of Voters' service, and how likely they were to serve in a future election. The results generally indicate positive evaluations by poll workers. In particular, when asked to rate the overall experience of serving in the November 2018 election, 84% of respondents gave an excellent or good rating. Moreover, 92% of poll workers who filled out the survey think the Registrar of Voters provided excellent or good services. Finally, 87% of respondents reported that they would likely or very likely serve in a future election. Among poll workers who were unlikely or very unlikely to serve in a future election, a majority described the problem to be the long hours. While poll workers can choose to work either the morning or the evening shift according to the Registrar of Voters, some poll workers may be unaware of this or underestimate the workload.

3.6　What Did We Learn?

In this section, we presented an account of how we built, deployed, and analyzed a large-scale postelection voter experience survey. We demonstrated that our voter experience survey enabled us to: identify important problems with registration that may have affected voters' ability to cast their ballots as intended; measure their confidence about their votes being counted correctly; and gauge the level of various concerns regarding election integrity. Our survey implementation and analysis provided a template for election administrators and researchers to evaluate the performance of election administration in future elections, incorporating the best practices from survey methodology research.

This survey yielded a wealth of useful information, both for our team and the OCROV. In conclusion, our voter experience survey indicates that in the 2018 general elections, there were very few problems for vote-by-mail, early, and Election Day voters. Our analyses indicate that most Orange County voters had good experiences voting and were strongly confident in the integrity of the 2018 elections in their county – impressive given the broader context of an election environment that was quite competitive, had strong voter turnout, and took place in a very large election jurisdiction. This is consistent with the results from Section 2, where we found that our social media monitoring tool produced very few reports of election problems in 2018 in Orange County.

Today, survey methodology is constantly evolving, both in response to the development of new communications technologies and in response to changing patterns of behavior. In the future, our team will focus on methodologies for sampling likely respondents, in particular for measuring low-incidence administrative or technological problems, and for minimizing nonresponse rates. We are studying innovative ways to ask registered voters questions about their voting experiences, in particular question formats that might make them feel more comfortable truthfully revealing their assessments and evaluations of their voting experience. Innovations like these will improve our ability to use survey methods to evaluate election integrity.

4   Election Auditing and Statistical Forensics

4.1   Auditing and Statistical Forensics

After the election, administrators begin the process of accounting for all of the materials used (for example, reconciling voted, voided, and unused ballots), verifying ballots cast by mail and provisional ballots, and tabulating or tallying the results. Once officials have accounted for all of the election's materials, as well as having verified that all valid ballots have been included in the tabulation, election officials certify and announce the final election results, usually within a few weeks after Election Day.[22] Given the complexity of election

---

[22] The exact schedule and procedures for postelection reconciliation, tallying, and certification vary considerably across counties and states in the United States a reflection of the rights that states retain under the US Constitution to regulate their elections (Article 1, Section 4).

administration and importance of assuring the integrity of the voting process in the United States, election officials and students of elections have devised a number of methodologies for confirming the accuracy of a reported election's outcome.

In the world of election administration, the primary methodology for confirming an election is a postelection ballot audit. Postelection ballot audits can confirm a reported election result, verify that ballot tabulation procedures and technologies are functioning as expected, and detect election tampering and fraud. If postelection audits confirm the reported outcome of an election, they represent one of the primary ways to boost the confidence of voters and stakeholders in the integrity of election administration and technology.

These postelection ballot audits are typically conducted by election officials, in the days and weeks immediately following Election Day. In the next subsections of this section we will dig further into the details of how to conduct these audits. It is important to note that these types of ballot audits are usually done by election officials themselves, as they require the use of cast ballots in a recent election. While there are a variety of different procedures, most often a sample of ballots are retabulated, with the results of the new tabulation compared with the original tally. If discrepancies arise between the audited tabulation and the original tabulation, the discrepancies can be further studied to determine their cause. The results of this analysis determine the potential consequence for the eventual certification of the election.

In contrast to ballot audits, we term the second class of postelection auditing methodologies election forensics. These differ from postelection ballot audits in two important ways. First, election forensics are often much broader in scope: postelection ballot audits are largely focused on confirming the tabulation of a recent election using samples of ballots cast in that election; election forensics focus on other election statistics like voter participation, spoiled and voided ballots, residual or uncounted ballots, and votes cast for specific candidates or issues. Second, election forensics do not typically use only individual cast ballots; rather, they use summaries or aggregations of elections data – precinct statistics, or county or other low levels of political geography. Thus, election forensics are often conducted by scholars and stakeholders, using data that are made available to the public after the conclusion of an election. In our project, we focused on two important forensic methods. First, we collected elections data and studied the distributions of important election statistics, especially turnout, and used statistical outlier analyses to detect issues for further investigation. Second, we used other forensic analyses of data from the postelection canvass, to examine the data for different potential issues. These analyses included comparing the election outcomes for many of the important

Table 4 Postelection audits in the United States, 2019

None	Traditional		Risk-limiting	Other
Alabama	Alaska	Arizona	Colorado	Idaho
Arkansas	California	Connecticut	Rhode Island	Indiana
Delaware	District of Columbia	Florida	Virginia	Nebraska
Georgia	Hawaii	Illinois		North Dakota
Louisiana	Iowa	Kansas		South Carolina
Maine	Kentucky	Maryland		Wyoming
Mississippi	Massachusetts	Michigan		
New Hampshire	Minnesota	Missouri		
· Oklahoma	Montana	Nevada		
South Dakota	New Jersey	New Mexico		
	New York	North Carolina		
	Ohio	Oregon		
	Pennsylvania	Tennessee		
	Texas	Utah		
	Vermont	Washington		
	West Virginia	Wisconsin		
10	32		3	6

Note: Data from National Council of State Legislatures, May 2019. See text for explanation of categories and exceptions.

races in Orange County, between close and not very close races and between this election cycle and previous election cycles, and by comparing election results from Orange County to those of other jurisdictions. All of these comparisons allow us to find any anomalies in Orange County that might require further examination. As we discuss in the conclusion to this section, in the 2018 election in Orange County, we did not deploy the third set of forensic methodologies for election anomaly detection: that is, more advanced statistical and machine learning methods.

4.2   Postelection Auditing

Currently in the United States, states have many different procedures used in conducting postelection ballot audits. According to information collected by the National Council of State Legislators (May 2019), most states currently require the use of some type of traditional, or "fixed-percentage," postelection ballot audit (see Table 4). A total of 32 states rely on some type of fixed-percentage postelection ballot audit (New Mexico uses a tiered auditing system based on the margin of victory). Going into the 2020 presidential election cycle, only three states require risk-limiting audits (Colorado, Rhode Island, and Virginia), while Ohio and Washington allow counties to conduct such audits. California is likely to allow for risk-limiting audits in 2020. Six states have some other type of auditing system, and ten states have no requirements for postelection ballot auditing.

Orange County is an excellent case for discussing postelection ballot audits, as in 2018 it conducted two different types of audits, both of which we will examine in the first part of this section. Since the 1960s, California's election code has required that counties conduct a "One Percent Manual Tally."[23] This postelection ballot audit is conducted during the canvass period, and each county's election official is required to sample 1% of precincts in the jurisdiction. After collecting this sample, officials manually tally the ballots cast in person on Election Day and by mail (not including provisional ballots) in a public venue. The purpose of a fixed-percentage postelection ballot audit procedure, like the one required in California, is to confirm that the procedures and technologies used to tally ballots are functioning as expected.

The election official is to pick the precincts to tally randomly, but has the discretion to include additional precincts, and vote-by-mail or provisional ballots. Otherwise, regulations are largely silent on the specifics of how to conduct the tally. The outcome of this procedure requires that the election official reports on the results of the tally as part of the certification of the election. Specifically, the current regulation requires that:

> This report shall identify any discrepancies between the machine count and the manual tally and a description of how each of these discrepancies was resolved. In resolving a discrepancy involving a vote recorded by means of a punchcard voting system or by electronic or electromechanical vote tabulating devices, the voter-verified paper audit trail shall govern if there is a discrepancy between it and the electronic record.

There is no requirement that detailed reports of the 1% manual tally be made available to the public.

Recently, California's election code was amended to allow counties to conduct pilot "risk-limiting audits." As defined in the election code:[24]

> "Risk-limiting audit" means a post-election process that involves hand-to-eye, human inspection of ballots in such a manner that if a full manual tally of all the ballots cast in the contest would show different outcomes than the results reported by the voting system, there is at most a five percent chance that the post-election process will not lead

---

[23] The current regulations for this requirement are in California Election Code 15360. For details on the history of the 1% manual tally in California, and on how counties conduct it, see Hall (2008a, 2008b).

[24] See California Election Code 15365.

to such a full manual tally. If this post-election process does lead to a full manual tally, the winner or winners according to that full manual tally replace the winner or winners as reported by the voting system if they differ.

This is a very different type of postelection ballot audit, designed not to confirm the appropriating functionality of tallying procedures and equipment, but to provide statistical confirmation of the accuracy of the reported election outcome. California's election code also requires that counties that conduct these pilot risk-limited audits do so in a "public and observable process," and that they "publish a report on the results of the risk-limiting audit in the certification of the official canvass of the vote."

It is important to note that neither of these postelection ballot auditing procedures necessarily constitutes a "recount" of a contest in a particular election. For example, in California, election recounts are part of an entirely different section of the state's election code than postelection ballot auditing procedures (California Election Code 15600-15649). Recounts are typically conducted for a particular race or contest; that is, for a particular candidate or ballot measure, and are only conducted upon request. The state's election code provides provisions for election officials themselves to request a recount of ballots in a precinct (for example, if ballots in a precinct might have been miscounted, or if for some reason a precinct's results are anomalous); recounts can also be requested by voters, courts, the Governor, and the Secretary of State. The conceptual difference between a recount and a postelection ballot audit is that the recounts focus on apparent anomalies in *specific* contests or candidate's votes. Recounts are often triggered by a request and usually include all ballots cast. In contrast, postelection ballot audits are a routine procedure, typically covering a fraction of the precincts or ballots cast in an election.

In the 2018 election cycle, Orange County both performed the required 1% manual tally and conducted pilot risk-limiting ballot audits. This gives us data that we can use to compare the two types of postelection ballot audit, and to better understand how these procedures fit into a holistic and ecological evaluation of the integrity of an election. In the next two subsections of Section 4, we dig a bit more deeply into the two primary types of postelection ballot audit, and discuss what can be learned from each.

4.2.1   Fixed Percentage Audits

There have been few systematic studies of fixed-percentage election auditing results. The one comprehensive study we are aware of used data from Los Angeles County, when the County used prescored punch cards and then transitioned to the InkaVote system (elections in 2000–2005; Alvarez, Katz, et al.,

2012). In that study, admittedly focusing on very different types of voting systems than currently used in Orange County, the authors found that when ballots were tallied manually, the hand counts almost always counted more ballots than the original machine tally, albeit with only slight deviations. The authors argue that this result most likely arises due to issues specific to prescored punch cards and the "re-inking" of InkaVote ballots in Los Angeles County.

Again, in 2018 Orange County used very different voting technology from the voting system that generated the data used in that paper (the Hart E-Slate, with voter-verified paper audit trails), so we do not expect to find the same sort of results in the 2018 general election 1% manual tally data from Orange County. OCROV selected 16 precincts for a full manual tally, and 58 precincts for a partial manual tally of a specific contest on the ballot. In total, 57,178 ballots were included in the manual tally.

There were only two variances found in the 2018 Orange County general election manual tally. As written in the report provided by OCROV to the Secretary of State:[25]

Precinct 32101 had 5 additional ballots on the Voter Verifiable Paper Audit Trail that were not initially tallied. The discrepancy was researched, and it was determined that the selections were printed on the paper audit trail for the voter, but not ultimately cast on the JBC. The voters and the poll workers were notified by the voting system that the ballots were not cast, and the voters were given replacement ballots which were subsequently voted.
Precinct 49335 had 3 votes for a qualified write-in candidate in the City of San Juan Capistrano Member, City Council, District 3 that were manually resolved as undervotes during the ballot scanning process, but were given as votes to the candidate in the manual tally.

Thus, the 1% manual tally, as an example of a fixed percentage audit, is informative. From the 74 precincts that were fully or partially tallied after the November 2018 general election in Orange County, only these two variances were found. Both, minor in scope, were easily resolved. Neither indicated any significant issues with election procedures nor with technologies in the election, providing additional evidence that the election was conducted with integrity.

4.2.2 Variable Percentage Audits

In recent years, the risk-limiting audit (RLA) has been a widely discussed variable percentage auditing process, which has recently been implemented in a number of states (see Table 4). The RLA differs from a fixed-percentage audit,

---

[25] Provided by personal communication from the Orange County Registrar of Voters, Neal Kelley, May 25, 2019.

both in terms of the goal and methodology. The goal of an RLA is confirm that the initial ballot tally identified the correct winners. The RLA has been described by Lindeman and Stark (2012) as:

an "intelligent" incremental recount that stops when the audit provides sufficiently strong evidence that a full hand count would confirm the original (voting system) outcome. As long as the audit does not yield sufficiently strong evidence, more ballots are manually inspected, potentially progressing to a full hand tally of all the ballots.

There are two types of RLAs (Lindeman & Stark, 2012): ballot-polling and comparison risk-limiting audits. A particular jurisdiction's specific choice of RLA depends largely on that jurisdiction's election administration system. In locations where the election administration tallies ballots and can report vote counts for individual ballots or small clusters of ballots, it is possible to conduct a comparison RLA. Where the ballot tabulation system cannot report results for individual ballots or clusters of ballots, the ballot-polling RLA is used, usually requiring a sample of additional ballots. The ballot-polling RLA was used by OCROV in their 2018 pilots (as we will discuss in more detail later in this section), with the number of sampled ballots needed dependent upon the total number of ballots cast, the vote margin in the contest or contests being audited, and the risk limit set by the auditor.[26] In general, the greater the number of ballots cast, the closer the contest margins, or the lower the risk limit, the greater the number of ballots the ballot-polling audit will need to sample in order to confirm that the reported outcome was correct. Readers interested in the nuances of these two types of RLA are encouraged to consult the literature (e.g., Lindeman & Stark, 2012).

Because the ballot tabulation system used by OCROV could not accommodate the tallying of individual ballots, in 2018 the Registrar conducted a pilot study using ballot-polling audits. These were done in both the June 2018 primary and November 2018 general elections, in conjunction with the traditional 1% manual hand tally.

OCROV conducted their 2018 post-primary RLA in two phases – one immediately after the primary, but before the final tabulation of all valid ballots was complete; the other later in the postelection process, after the final tally of ballots was complete.[27]

---

[26] A useful tool for simulating quantities like the total number of ballots that will likely be sampled for a ballot-polling audit is available online, www.stat.berkeley.edu/~stark/Vote/ballotPollTools.htm.

[27] OCROV conducted the 2018 primary election RLA in two phases in order to determine if it could perform the RLA early in the postelection cycle, before all of the ballots have been tallied, during the immediate postelection canvass period. However, conducting an RLA is resource-intensive, requiring the allocation of a large number of personnel, who early in the postelection

The Registrar decided to focus these RLA efforts on three races – the Orange County Assessor, Auditor-Controller, and Clerk-Recorder. In the 2018 primary, there were 635,224 ballots cast, out of a total registered voter population of 1,481,881 (turnout in the primary was 43% of registered voters). The three races selected for the RLA were far down the ballot, below the statewide races, federal and state legislative races, and a handful of other county races. None of the races were very close: among the three candidates in the County Assessor race, Parrish received 69% of votes cast, relative to Ramirez at 17.4% and Epstein at 13.5%. In the County Auditor-Controller race, Wollery received 74.3% of the ballots cast, compared to Smart's 25.7%; the County Clerk Recorder margin was similar, with Nguyen getting 79.1% to Rocco's 20.9%. Given that these were not close elections, and that the Registrar set the risk margin for the RLA at 20%, very few ballots needed to be manually counted for the June 2018 RLA pilot: only 180.[28] Following the procedures OCROV developed for the 2018 pilot RLA, those ballots were sampled and the outcomes of those three races were confirmed (Orange County Registrar of Voters, 2019).

For the November 2018 general election, OCROV selected three races to audit: the County District Attorney, and the US House elections in Districts 45 and 48. Both of the US House races had very, very close margins of victory – in the 45th race, Porter beat the incumbent Walters 52% to 48%, and in the 48th, challenger Rouda won over incumbent Rohrabacher 54% to 46%. The closeness of these two races, and the greater number of ballots cast in the 2018 general election in Orange County, meant that the ballot-polling RLA would likely require a greater sample of ballots than was sampled in the primary election. The Registrar determined an expected sample size of 16,000 ballots for the November 2018 RLA pilot; that number was so great that OCROV used a different stopping rule in November, which was to stop the audit when it hit this risk limit (20%) or when 1,000 ballots had been tallied. This revised stopping rule for the RLA was deemed necessary because of resource constraints.[29]

---

canvass period are needed for other tasks. As the OCROV report concluded, "The disadvantage, which was discovered while performing the process, is that it requires additional coordination of resources. As an example, the office's resources that are dedicated to processing and tallying ballots are not available to assist with the audit process" (Orange County Registrar of Voters, 2019, p. 16).

[28] The 20% risk margin implies that there is an 80% chance that if the original tabulation outcome is incorrect, the RLA will produce the correct outcome.

[29] OCROV explained in their report, "While the risk-limiting tool provided an expected sample size of 16,000 ballots to audit before meeting the risk limit, the Registrar of Voters decided to stop the audit once the risk limit was met for all contexts or once 1,000 ballots had been counted. This was because the risk-limiting audit pilot was simultaneously conducted with the mandated 1% manual tally, which required a large portion of the offices' resources" (Orange County Registrar of Voters, 2019, p. 16).

After auditing 540 ballots for the District Attorney (which was not as close as the two Congressional general elections), the RLA hit the 20% risk limit and the original outcome was confirmed. However, the risk limit was not met for the two Congressional elections after 1,000 ballots were audited, and thus the RLA had to be stopped before it could confirm the outcome of those two races.

4.2.3   What Can We Learn from Postelection Ballot Audits?

Postelection ballot audits are instructive tools that can confirm that the ballot tabulation system has worked as expected (in the case of a fixed-percentage ballot audit) or that the original outcome of a race is likely to be correct (in the case of a variable-percentage ballot audit like the RLA). In the case of Orange County in 2018, as the County carried out parallel fixed-percentage and variable-percentages postelection ballot audits, and they produced (generally) confirmatory outcomes, these procedures help increase confidence about the integrity of the ballot tabulation process and technology, and the correctness of the reported outcome (for one contest).

  That said, while postelection ballot audits are useful for confirming the integrity of an election, they are limited in what they can tell us about the integrity of the entire election process; they only examine the tabulation of ballots, and the correctness of the election outcome, and can generally find anomalies in that single stage of the election process. If there were larger-scale inaccuracies in the voter registration file, significant problems experienced by voters in polling locations on Election Day, or if there was any fraud that changed the original paper ballots, a postelection ballot audit would be unlikely to detect these or similar problems. Furthermore, postelection ballot audits cannot detect situations where large numbers of eligible voters may have been removed from the registration lists, either by administrative error or fraud.[30]

  Consider, as another example, what would happen if operatives decided to engage in voting-by-mail fraud of a sufficient scale to have altered the outcome of an election like the 45th House race in Orange County, where adding a mere 12,000 votes could have flipped the outcome of that important and contested election (or thrown it into doubt). There were just over 400 precincts in this House district in 2018, which means that the operatives would need to add about 30 votes for their candidate in each precinct. Were they able to obtain and return three dozen absentee ballots which would add votes for their candidate

---

[30] In the June 2018 primary election in Los Angeles County (CA), the names of 118,521 of those eligible to vote, across 4,357 polling locations in the county, were removed from voter lists by administrative error before the election (www.lavote.net/docs/rrcc/news-releases/06052018_E-Day-Release.pdf).

to the final ballot tally, neither the fixed-percentage nor the variable-percentage postelection ballot tally would necessarily detect such fraud; rather, manually tallying ballots would simply replicate the reported results. Of course, election fraud of this scale would be quite difficult to perpetrate, and could potentially be detected in other ways – discrepancies between signatures on file and on the absentee envelope, for example. The point here is that postelection ballot audits would not necessarily detect election fraud that affects the original ballots tallied.

Finally, in most cases, postelection and performance auditing is conducted exclusively by election officials, as they are the only actors that typically have access to the sensitive materials necessary for the audit (for example, the original ballots). Thus, a skeptic could point out the difficulty in wholly trusting the results of a postelection ballot audit conducted by election officials: the audit is being conducted by the organization being audited. This creates a potential conflict of interest, and because of this conflict, there is a lot of interest in developing auditing techniques that can be used by independent third parties who do not have the same interest in confirming reported election results. Thus, for an independent confirmation of election integrity, having auditing done outside of the direct control of the election jurisdiction could be important.

4.3   Election Forensics

Of course, in order to determine whether an election was administered with integrity, more needs to be done than just confirming that ballot tabulations are correct. Thus, a number of other statistical methods for auditing elections have been developed, methods that can be conducted independently of election officials and that can help confirm the integrity of an election. Often these approaches are called "election forensics," though within that general category there is a wide variety of statistical techniques and aspects of an election that can be studied. In general, election forensics techniques are a specific class of statistical anomaly detection methods (Chandola, Banerjee, & Kumar, 2009), tools that look for oddities or outliers in datasets, and that can then be further investigated to determine whether these are the result of misreported data, administrative error, or potential election fraud. Statistical anomaly detection methods are widely used to detect fraud in financial data and credit card transactions, as well as to identify potential criminal activity and national security risks (Chandola et al., 2009).

When it comes to election forensics methods, these are a specific class of statistical anomaly detection methods, usually applied to precinct-by-precinct voter turnout or candidate vote shares data (though as we report in other sections of this Element, they can be used with voter registration data as well as social media monitoring). Some of these election forensics methods concentrate on finding anomalies in election statistics, like irregularities in digits (Beber & Scacco, 2012; Mebane, 2008, 2011) or lumpy reporting of election results using only certain digits (Rozenas, 2017). Others have looked for anomalies in the statistical distributions of quantities such as turnout and vote shares (Myakgov, Ordeshook, & Shaikin, 2009). More complex modeling approaches have been deployed to look for outliers, using regression models, regression trees, and machine learning ensembles (Alvarez & Katz, 2008; Cantú & Saiegh, 2011; Levin, Pomares, & Alvarez, 2016; Montgomery et al., 2015). For a summary of recent academic research in this area see Levin et al. (2016).

Here we focus on the use of statistical distribution tests, in particular using visualizations of the bivariate and univariate distributions of important election outcomes like voter turnout and candidate vote shares, measured at the precinct level. In our 2018 election integrity study in Orange County, we decided to utilize these methods, for a number of reasons. First, we did not have a great deal of past election returns data, at the precinct level, that we could use for modeling or machine learning anomaly detection – those methods require the use of historical data to predict expected turnout or vote shares. Second, we wanted forensics that we could produce quickly, and we found it relatively easy to obtain Orange County precinct-level turnout and statements of vote data during the postelection period. Third, we wanted forensics that were easy for nonexperts to understand, and as we will show in the next section, statistical distribution tests are straightforward to produce, transparent, and quite informative for election observers, officials, and the public.

In this section, we will focus on two important forensic methods. First, we examine the statistical distributions of important elections data, especially turnout, and will use statistical outlier analyses to detect issues for further investigation. Second, we took a series of deeper dives into the data from the postelection canvass, to examine the data for different potential issues. These analyses included comparing the election outcomes for many of the important races in Orange County, between close and not very close races and between this election cycle and previous election cycles, and by comparing election results from Orange County to those in other jurisdictions. These studies allow us to find anomalies in Orange County that might require further examination. We discuss both approaches in the next part of this section.

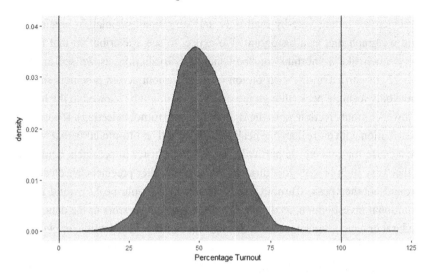

Figure 12 Hypothetical precinct-level turnout distribution

4.3.1   Turnout Forensics

Election forensics are useful for finding anomalies in elections data, as they can help diagnose administrative or procedural issues, technological problems, or even potential malfeasance. Often, however, detailed and granular data are not available to researchers or the public until after an election has been completed and winners have been declared. While forensic tools are useful when an election has been concluded (in particular, to help improve the process or technology for future elections), in order to produce timely and actionable recommendations to election officials in the immediate aftermath of an election, data must be made available for forensic analysis during the postelection canvass period.

Luckily, Orange County provides the exact type of data necessary for post-election forensics. OCROV releases detailed daily reports on voter turnout and vote totals, by precinct, as they proceed with tabulation. These reports are published on the OCROV website, in PDF form. Our task was therefore relatively straightforward: obtain the daily precinct turnout reports (we will discuss vote share analysis from the Statement of Vote reports in the next subsection), scrape the data from the PDF reports, process them, and analyze the data using graphical methods.

In Figure 12 we give a hypothetical example of what we expect to see in our graphical analyses of precinct-level voter turnout in Orange County. We estimate the percentage of registered voters who turned out to vote in each precinct (excluding vote-by-mail only and very small population precincts), and we graph that as a histogram. We expect to see a distribution that looks very much like a "normal" or "bell-shaped" distribution, as we see in Figure 12. In particular, the distribution of voter turnout across precincts should have only a single peak (though the distribution might be skewed to the left in a lower-turnout election, or to the right in a higher-turnout election). If we see a distribution with more than one peak (which we call "multi-modal"), that would be a cause for concern, in particular if we see a cluster of precincts reporting either very high or very low turnout, while most other precincts are clustered around another peak. Turnout histograms with multiple peaks would merit additional investigation, as that can be an indication of errors in the data, procedural or technological issues in the administration of the election, or election tampering.

The other diagnostic that we use arises from the very nature of the statistics that we are graphing. We are estimating the percentage of registered voters who cast ballots in the election (where the numerator for each day's reporting is the cumulative number of ballots tallied to date). While we will see the numerator increase during the tabulation of ballots after the election, thus shifting the distribution to the right, we should never see precincts reporting turnout percentages either above 100%, or below 0%. If we see precincts that are reporting percentage turnout that are outside these natural bounds for a percentage, we then know that there is something that needs further investigation – either the data are being misreported, there were procedural or technological issues, or perhaps there was some issue with the integrity of the election. By producing these analytics while the tallying is still occurring, we can produce very helpful intelligence for election administrators; if we find anomalies in the data, they can investigate those particular concerns before the election is certified.

The 2018 general election was held on November 6, 2018 – and our first analysis of the precinct turnout data used the report made available on November 8, 2018. We did not analyze data reported on November 6 or 7, as our qualitative observations of the election indicated that there may have been a large number of late-arriving vote-by-mail and provisional ballots, causing early turnout reports to potentially be noisy.

The first histogram that we produced using the November 8, 2018 precinct turnout data is shown in Figure 13. There are a number of important observations regarding the graphed distribution of turnout data from Orange County shown in this figure. First, generally, the distribution appears similar to a "normal" or "bell-shaped" distribution, with a slight degree of skewness toward the lower bound. Second, the distribution appears to only have one peak; countywide turnout at the point this report was released was 44%. Third, we do not see

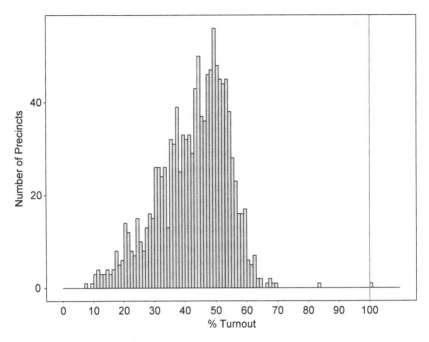

Figure 13 Turnout distribution: November 8, 2018

many outliers in the precinct turnout distribution; only two precincts appear to report turnout that is outside of the general distribution. The red vertical line in the figure is at 100% turnout, which helps to show that one of these precincts was reporting a turnout of greater than 100%.

When we found these two outliers – and keep in mind that there are only two outliers out of over 1000 polling locations – we dug into the data to identify the irregularities, passing the information along to OCROV for additional investigation.

The first outlier investigated, reporting turnout of 83.23% at this early stage in the postelection period, was precinct 38083, a precinct using a polling location at an elementary school in Laguna Hills. This precinct was consolidated with another precinct, 38312. In Orange County, it is common for two precincts to share the same polling location, as long as the voters in both precincts have the same ballot style. Precinct 38083 is relatively small, with 465 registered voters, though 387 ballots were reported cast by voters from that precinct. On the other hand, precinct 38312 is relatively large, with 1086 registered voters, and at that point in time reported 484 votes cast.

We noted the discrepancy in turnout rates between these two precincts, in the same area, voting at the same polling place: precinct 38083 was reporting 83%

turnout, while 38312 was reporting 45% turnout. It is quite unlikely that there would be such a dramatic difference in turnout, in the same election, by voters from very similar geographic areas. What appears to have occurred in this precinct was an administrative error by precinct workers – given that the two precincts were consolidated into the one location (using the same ballot style), it is most likely that some of the voters from precinct 38312 were incorrectly recorded as having voted in precinct 38083. A similar anomaly was noted by a study like this in the June 2018 primary, and we confirmed with OCROV that this administrative mixup is the most likely explanation for this outlier.

The second outlier is precinct 25382, which on November 8, 2018 was reporting that 674 ballots were cast, in a precinct with 670 registered voters. This precinct was located in a residential community in Laguna Woods, a community where there were a number of other polling locations. After we identified this outlier and notified OCROV, their forensic investigation produced evidence that there was an administrative explanation for this outlier. In 2018, Orange County's legacy voting system was the one originally produced by Hart InterCivic, the "eSlate." This is an electronic voting system, with a voter-verified paper audit trail. In each polling place, the eSlate voting devices that voters use are connected to a central unit called a "Judge's Booth Controller" (or JBC). It seems that the JBC assigned to precinct 25382 was used at another precinct (25234), while the JBC for precinct 25234 was at precinct 25382, but was not used, and no votes were recorded on the JBC assigned to precinct 25382. Further analysis by OCROV of the votes cast at each polling place confirmed that this was the likely explanation for this turnout anomaly.

Interestingly, as additional ballots were tabulated after the 2018 general election in Orange County, the distribution of turnout changed. For comparison, in Figure 14 we show the turnout distribution from data reported on November 30, 2018. Notice that the distribution of turnout across precincts has shifted to the right – and countywide on November 30, 2018, reported turnout at 71%. The distribution has lost some of the leftward skewness that it had on November 8, has a clear central tendency, and has a relatively smooth distribution. The two outliers remain, though, with additional cast ballots in each of the two outlying precincts being added to each precinct's numerator, so that by November 30, 2018 both were reported at well above 100%.

It is important to put these findings in the right context. In the final Statement of Votes for the 2018 general election, Orange County had 1,546 voting precincts.[31] That only two of those voting precincts reported anomalous results,

---

[31] www.ocvote.com/fileadmin/live/gen2018/sov.pdf

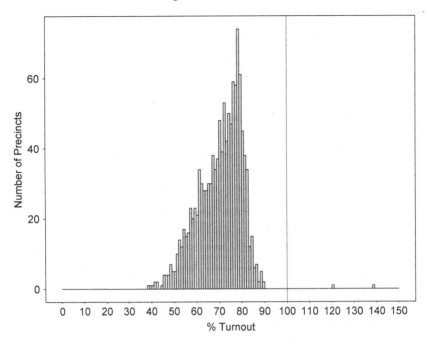

Figure 14 Turnout distribution: November 30, 2018

and that the anomalous results have administrative explanations, is an important finding. Furthermore, OCROV found the work that our team did with these forensic studies very helpful: our original forensic findings using the data from November 8 allowed OCROV to investigate the anomalous precincts, and our final report on turnout forensics using the November 30 data was useful when word began to circulate online and in the media about the issue of precincts reporting greater than 100% turnout. Knowing that these anomalies existed, and having investigated them, when these questions arose about these precincts, OCROV was able to quickly and effectively deal with them.

4.3.2   Vote Share Forensics

In our 2018 work in Orange County, we also applied similar types of visual election forensics to other postelection data, in particular the reported candidate vote shares. OCROV also posts periodic updates, beginning on Election Day and continuing until the postelection tabulation is completed, of precinct-by-precinct vote totals for all measures on the ballot. These reports are posted on the OCROV website, in PDF reports that we obtained, parsed for the data contained in each report, and then subjected to additional analysis.

The first step in our analysis is to look at candidate vote shares for a number of countywide races, especially the state constitutional officers – Governor, Lt. Governor, Controller, and Secretary of State. We search these vote share data in both the primary and general elections for anomalies. We have similar expectations for candidate vote shares to those already discussed with respect to turnout forensics: when studying the univariate distribution of any candidate's vote share in a histogram, we expect that those distributions should be single-peaked, and should have a generally smooth distribution (like the "normal" or "bell-shaped" distribution). Thus we expect to see relatively smooth and single-peaked distributions; if we see multi-modal distributions, or distributions with extreme outliers, those would be flagged for further study and investigation.

The second basic visualization we use for candidate vote share forensics is to look at the joint distribution of candidate vote shares by precinct turnout. Here again, we expect to see joint distributions between candidate vote shares and precinct turnout that do not have extreme outliers, and that the joint distributions do not have multiple clusters of precincts in the examined scatterplots. When we look at the joint distribution between candidate vote shares and turnout in scatterplots, anomalies that would call for further investigation would manifest as extreme outliers (say precincts where we see very high reported turnout and very high proportions of votes going to one candidate).

The other type of anomaly that we are looking for in the scatterplots of candidate vote shares and precinct turnout are multiple clusters of outlier precincts. An irregular joint distribution in one of these scatterplots would take the form of multiple clusters. For example, in a vote share by precinct turnout scatterplot we might find that much of a candidate's vote comes from moderate-turnout precincts. However, if this same scatterplot reveals a clear cluster of very-high-turnout precincts where the candidate receives a very large proportion of votes, these clusters would require further study and investigation.

The first of these studies that we produced for the 2018 general election used data from the November 15, 2018 precinct report of the Statement of Votes, issued by OCROV. We downloaded the PDF version of the report from the OCROV website and parsed it to obtain the data on votes cast in each race, for each candidate, and by precinct, as well the turnout in each precinct. As with our turnout studies reported above, we dropped precincts with very small numbers of registered voters (which typically are all-mail precincts); we also dropped the two precincts with very high reported turnout (precincts 25382 and 38083, as discussed in the previous subsection). From the raw data, we compute the vote shares for each candidate (their percentage of votes in each precinct in the current tabulation, of total ballots cast in the precinct). Note again that

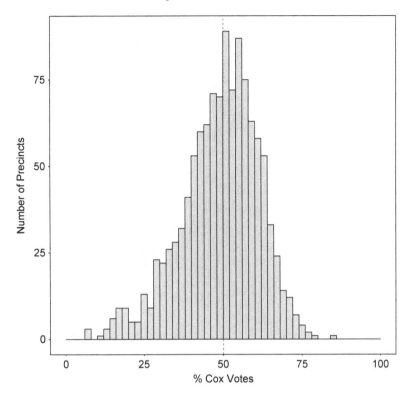

Figure 15 Cox vote share distribution: November 15, 2018

this analysis uses data from the November 15, 2018 tabulation report – so these data are not final, and do not reflect the final vote totals for the election.

We provide the histograms of candidate vote shares for the two gubernatorial candidates in the general election, from the very top of the ballot in Orange County. The first analysis shows the univariate distribution of candidate vote shares for the Republican candidate, John H. Cox, in Figure 15. A similar graph for the Democratic candidate, Gavin Newsom, is provided in Figure 16.

Keep in mind that we are looking for smooth and single-peaked distributions of candidate vote shares in these two analyses, without indication of a significant number of outlier precincts (very low or very high candidate vote shares). Examination of Figures 15 and 16 shows what we expect. The histogram of the Republican candidate's vote share (Cox, Figure 15) is single-peaked and smooth, with only a slight degree of skewness to the left (a small proportion of precincts with less than 25% votes going to Cox). The histogram for the Democratic candidate's vote share (Newsom), in Figure 16, is similar – single-peaked, smooth, with a small degree of skewness to the right. These two figures

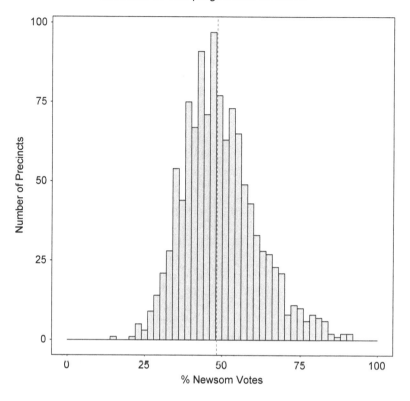

Figure 16 Newsom vote share distribution: November 15, 2018

show no indication of outliers or anomalies needing further study. Also, at the same time that we did this analysis, we also looked at similar histograms for candidate vote shares in a number of the other state constitutional officer races; in those analyses, we saw no evidence of anomalies or outliers needing further investigation.

Next, we dug further into the SOV data, looking at the joint distributions of gubernatorial candidate vote shares and precinct-by-precinct turnout. As we noted earlier, when we look at the joint distributions of these covariates, anomalies or outliers in the data will appear in the scatterplots as joint distributions that are not linear, or which have bi- or multi-modality. We show these joint distributions in Figure 17.

·What we see in Figure 17 are two distinct clouds of points, with each point representing a precinct's vote share for one of the two candidates (Cox in red, Newsom in blue) and turnout. We have drawn a least-squares fit line to highlight the apparent linearity of the two joint distributions shown in the figure. For the Republican candidate Cox, we see a strong positive correlation in Orange

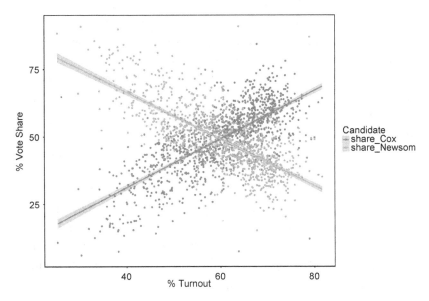

Figure 17 Gubernatorial candidate vote share by turnout: November 15, 2018

County; in precincts with higher turnout, he receives a greater share of the votes cast in the gubernatorial race. For the Democratic candidate Newsom, we see the opposite, a strongly negative relationship, as he receives a greater vote share in low-turnout precincts. Other than these two obvious correlation patterns, we do not see any evidence of anomalies in the joint distributions – the plotted distributions are relatively linear, and we do not see any signs of bi- or multi-modality in these data.

4.3.3 Split-Ticket Voting by Congressional District

In the immediate aftermath of the 2018 November general elections in Orange County, questions arose because of the relatively strong showing of Democratic candidates in a number of the US Congressional elections in the county. As Orange County has traditionally been a bastion of right-wing and Republican activism in Southern California, and given that Republican candidates like Cox performed well in Orange County, some wondered how some of the Republican Congressional candidates could have seemingly underperformed countywide Republican candidates like Cox.[32] Was it really the case that Orange County voters, who apparently had so consistently supported Republican statewide

---

[32] Cox ended up receiving 539,951 votes of a total 1,106,729 cast in Orange County's gubernatorial race, or about 48.8%.

and Congressional candidates in the past, would in 2018 vote for Democratic Congressional candidates? Would voters cast ballots for Republican statewide candidates, but for Democratic Congressional candidates?

Decades of research on American political behavior has reinforced the primacy of partisanship (Campbell et al., 1980). A voter's partisan identification is a strong predictor of how they will cast their ballots in any particular election; given the strength of the association between partisanship and voting behavior, we expect to see voters casting straight-party ballots in places where one party is strong, like Orange County.

That said, it is worth noting that by 2018, the Republican Party's strength in Orange County had diminished considerably. The October 10, 2000 Report on Registration issued by California's Secretary of State showed that 49.19% of the County's registered voters were Republican (to 32.15% Democratic). But by the October 22, 2018 Report on Registration, registration with the Republican Party had fallen to 34.72%, barely edging the Democratic registration rate in Orange County of 33.56%.

Also, research has shown that the power of partisanship, while still strong in the United States, is not all-consuming. American voters are known to ignore or downplay partisanship in their voting behavior, especially in situations where factors other than partisanship become salient in their decision making. For example, candidate personalities and experience, local issues, and other concerns might factor more heavily into voter decision making than party. This can lead voters to cast ballots for candidates of the party they identify with in some races, but on the same ballot to cast ballots for candidates of other parties – what political scientists call split-ticket voting (Alvarez & Schousen, 1993; Burden & Kimball, 2002).

Regarding the specific context of Orange County, we needed to consider the specific political situation in order to hypothesize whether we expected to find split-ticket voting. As noted earlier, even by 2018 Republicans had a slight registration edge in the County. The top-of-the-ticket gubernatorial race between Newsom and Cox did not spark a lot of campaign activity, so there was little to sway voters from simply casting a ballot for their party's candidate.

However, the US House races in Orange County represent quite a different story. In 2018, some of the most closely contested US Congressional elections occurred in Orange County, in particular in CA 39 and CA 45. Rival organizations heavily outspent Republican US House candidates in Orange County, and there was a great deal of campaign activity in the county by independent groups, especially those supporting Democratic House candidates. It is also important to note that some of the issues in play in the 2018 general election, like healthcare and the tax reform bill passed by Congress, may have favored

Table 5 Vote share by Congressional district in Orange County

	Overall	Governor				US House of Representatives			
	Ballots	DEM	REP	None	R-D	DEM	REP	None	R-D
CA38	5,809	49.5%	48.5%	1.9%	-1.0%	51.5%	44.5%	4.0%	-6.9%
CA39	162,126	46.1%	51.8%	2.1%	5.8%	48.1%	49.4%	2.4%	1.3%
CA45	312,700	48.5%	49.7%	1.8%	1.1%	50.8%	46.8%	2.4%	-4.0%
CA46	154,136	61.9%	35.1%	3.0%	-26.8%	66.4%	29.6%	4.0%	-36.7%
CA47	90,592	48.6%	48.7%	2.6%	0.1%	51.0%	44.2%	4.7%	-6.8%
CA48	303,973	46.9%	51.0%	2.1%	4.1%	51.9%	45.0%	3.0%	-6.9%
CA49	77,393	41.1%	57.4%	1.5%	16.3%	45.4%	52.1%	2.5%	6.7%

Democratic House candidates in Orange County. This part of the context indicates that Orange County voters could well have supported Democratic House candidates, especially in the competitive races, and that there might have been significant split-ticket voting for purely political reasons. Therefore, we may expect to find evidence of split-ticket voting in Orange County and not consider this an indication of anomalies or malfeasance.

Ideally, studying ticket-splitting would necessitate the use of individual-level ballot records. Unfortunately, to preserve the privacy of the act of voting, for the purposes of our study we did not have access to the individual-level ballot records. Thus, as in the previous section, we use readily available aggregated data, the precinct-by-precinct Statement of Votes (SOV) report.[33] We analyze the precinct-level data, looking for patterns in the aggregate data that will help us test whether there appear to be any anomalies in the vote shares for partisan candidates in different races in Orange County.

Our first look at the data is in Table 5, where we present party vote shares from the 2018 general election by Congressional race in Orange County. In the first column of the table, we give the total ballots cast in that race, followed by the votes cast for the Democratic and Republican candidates for governor. The second set of columns gives similar information for the partisan candidates in the specific Congressional race. The first important analysis is to compare the votes cast for Newsom relative to the votes cast for the Democratic Congressional candidate, as well as for Cox and the Republican Congressional candidate. In every Congressional race in Orange County, the Democratic Congressional candidate outperforms Newsom (the Democratic gubernatorial candidate); the overperformance ranges from 2% in CA 38 and CA 39 to over 5% in CA 48. For Republicans, we see that in every Congressional district in Orange County, the Republican gubernatorial candidate Cox outperforms

---

[33] www.ocvote.com/fileadmin/live/gen2018/sov.pdf

Republican House candidates. Cox's overperformance ranges from 2.4% in CA 39 to 6% in CA 48.

What do we learn from Table 5? In the 2018 general election in Orange County, the most contested House races were in CD 39, CD 45, and CD 49. Those were the races where concerns about ticket-splitting should be focused. Thus, if those districts had unusual levels of split-ticket voting, we'd expect those three districts to appear to have voting dynamics much different than the other US House races in the County. For example, we might expect to see strong Democratic candidate overperformance in those races, but to see the opposite in the less contested races, where split-ticket voting might not be as prevalent.

That's not what we see in the data shown in Table 5. Instead, the Democratic House candidates overperform relative to Newsom, and the Republican House candidates underperform relative to Cox, countywide, in all of the House races in Orange County. If there was a shift toward supporting Democratic House candidates in Orange County, that shift appears countywide, and is not limited to only the very competitive House races.

We further investigate the extent and magnitude of Republican Congressional candidates' underperformance by studying candidate vote share by precinct. For each precinct, we calculate the *Republican Congressional*

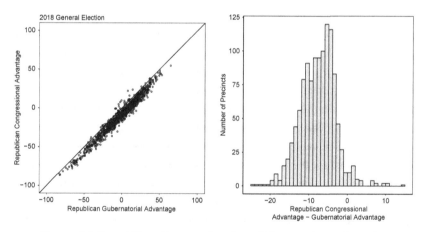

Figure 18 Republican Congressional candidates underperform the Republican Governor Candidate, John H. Cox, across precincts in Orange County

Note: The figure on the left displays Republican Congressional advantage (*y*-axis) and Republican gubernatorial advantage (*x*-axis) by precinct. The figure on the right displays the histogram of Republican Congressional advantage minus Republican gubernatorial advantage by precinct.

advantage as the candidate's vote share minus their Democratic counterpart's vote share.

We also calculate the *Republican gubernatorial advantage* as Cox's vote share minus Newsom's. The left panel of Figure 18 shows the scatterplot of Republican Congressional candidate advantage (*y*-axis) and Republican gubernatorial candidate advantage (*x*-axis) by precinct, with points falling on the 45-degree line (solid) when Republican Congressional candidates perform equally as well as the Republican gubernatorial candidate. Clearly, the performance of the Republican Congressional candidates is strongly correlated with Cox's performance at the precinct level. However, most points lie below that line (with a large number of them falling well below the 45-degree line), indicating that Republican Congressional candidates underperform the Republican gubernatorial candidate across most precincts in Orange County (in a large number of precincts by significant amounts). The right panel of Figure 18 shows a histogram of Republican Congressional advantage minus Republican gubernatorial advantage by precinct. Confirming our observation from the scatterplot, Republican Congressional candidates generally underperform the Republican gubernatorial candidate, John H. Cox, with a typical magnitude of Republican Congressional advantage minus Republican gubernatorial advantage between -4 and -12 percentage points.

Next, we look at the underperformance of Republican Congressional candidates separately for two contested races (CA 39 and CA 45) and five noncontested races (CA 38, CA 46, CA 47, CA 48, and CA 49).

As Table 5 shows, the Republican gubernatorial candidate, John H. Cox, wins 5.8% and 1.1% more votes than his Democratic competitor, Gavin Newsom, in CA 39 and CA 45 precincts in Orange County. Despite these advantages in the gubernatorial contest, Young Kim (Republican) wins only 1.3% more votes than Gil Cisneros (Democrat) in CA 39 precincts in Orange County, while Mimi Walters (Republican) is 4.0% short of votes compared to Katie Porter (Democrat) in CA 45 precincts in Orange County. These results amount to a lower Republican Congressional advantage than Republican gubernatorial advantage in these contested races, of 4.5% and 5.1% respectively.

Despite the underperformance in CA 39 and CA 45, Republican Congressional candidates underperform the Republican gubernatorial candidate, John H. Cox, *even more* in five noncontested races. The difference between the Republican Congressional advantage and the Republican gubernatorial advantage is 5.9% for CA 38, 6.9% for CA 47, 9.6% in CA 49, 9.9% in CA 46, and 11.0% in CA 48.

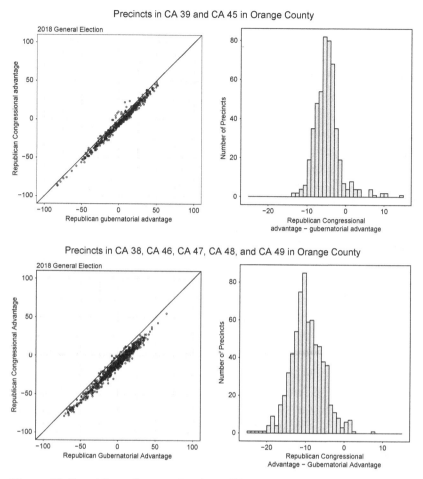

Figure 19 Republican Congressional candidates' underperformance is larger in precincts in contested Congressional districts in Orange County

Note: The figure on the left displays Republican Congressional advantage (*y*-axis) and Republican gubernatorial advantage (*x*-axis) by precinct. The figure on the right displays the histogram of Republican Congressional advantage minus Republican gubernatorial advantage by precinct.

Next, Figure 19 shows that for precincts with contested and noncontested Congressional races, respectively, the scatterplots and histograms are similar to those in Figure 18. Comparing the scatterplots, the points are more concentrated near the 45-degree line in the scatterplots for CA 39 and CA 45 precincts and farther away from the solid line for precincts in CA 38, CA 46, CA 47, CA 48, and CA 49. This pattern indicates that the Republican Congressional candidates underperform the Republican gubernatorial candidate, John H. Cox, more in noncontested races, and it is a general countywide phenomenon, not driven by a handful of anomalous precincts. Turning attention to the histograms, there is a clear left shift in the distribution of Republican Congressional advantage minus Republican gubernatorial advantage, when we move from contested races to noncontested ones. A typical magnitude of the Republican Congressional advantage minus the Republican gubernatorial advantage is between -4 and -8 percentage points for CA 39 and CA 45 precincts, and -9 and -13 percentage points for precincts in CA 38, CA 46, CA 47, CA 48, and CA 49.

Another way to look at ticket-splitting in Orange County is to examine whether the underperformance of the Republican Congressional candidates is limited to that county. So we conducted a similar analysis for Los Angeles County. The data we use in this analysis come from the official Statement of Votes that the Los Angeles County Registrar of Voters has made available on their website: www.lavote.net/docs/rrcc/svc/3861_svc_precinct _zbc.pdf?v=1.

In Table 6, we present party vote shares by Congressional district from Los Angeles County. We focus on 14 Congressional races with Democratic and Republican candidates.[34] As is clear from the table, in 12 out of 14 Congressional districts, the Democratic Congressional candidates outperform the Democratic gubernatorial candidate, Newsom, with the largest overperformance of 3% seen in CA 25. Meanwhile, Republican Congressional candidates perform worse than the Republican gubernatorial candidate, Cox, across Los Angeles County. The underperformance of Republican Congressional candidates is also large in magnitude, and is at least 3% for 11 out of 14 Congressional races.

Figure 20 presents a scatterplot and histogram similar to those in Figure 18, but for Los Angeles County. Since there are many more precincts in Los Angeles County than Orange County, we have more points in the scatterplot compared to Figure 18. But similar to what we saw for Orange County, the performance of the Republican Congressional candidates is strongly correlated with John H. Cox's performance at the precinct level. More importantly, Republican candidates similarly underperform the Republican gubernatorial candidate across most precincts in Los Angeles County even though the magnitude is somewhat smaller. The histogram in Figure 20 shows that the typical magnitude of Republican Congressional advantage minus Republican gubernatorial advantage was between -3 and -6 percentage points in Los Angeles County.

---

[34] Two Democratic candidates compete in CA 27 and CA 44. A Democratic candidate and a Green Party candidate compete in CA 34 and CA 40.

Table 6 Vote share by congressional district in Los Angeles County

	Overall					US House of Representatives			
		Governor							
	Ballots	DEM	REP	None	REP-DEM	DEM	REP	None	REP-DEM
CA 23	24,955	45.4%	51.9%	2.7%	6.5%	44.3%	51.1%	4.6%	6.8%
CA 25	198,801	51.3%	46.3%	2.5%	−5.0%	54.1%	43.1%	2.8%	−11.1%
CA 26	4,535	51.5%	46.3%	2.2%	−5.2%	54.1%	42.2%	3.7%	−11.9%
CA 28	262,298	73.5%	24.1%	2.4%	−49.4%	75.0%	20.7%	4.4%	−54.3%
CA 29	162,760	75.7%	21.6%	2.8%	−54.1%	76.6%	18.4%	5.0%	−58.2%
CA 30	271,454	68.4%	29.3%	2.3%	−39.0%	70.3%	25.4%	4.3%	−44.9%
CA 32	186,109	63.2%	33.8%	3.0%	−29.4%	64.9%	29.5%	5.6%	−35.4%
CA 33	327,578	66.1%	31.5%	2.4%	−34.6%	66.8%	28.6%	4.7%	−38.2%
CA 35	32,053	70.4%	26.4%	3.2%	−44.0%	72.1%	23.3%	4.7%	−48.8%
CA 37	249,502	84.0%	13.3%	2.6%	−70.7%	84.3%	10.3%	5.3%	−74.0%
CA 38	206,520	63.8%	33.3%	2.9%	−30.6%	65.8%	29.2%	5.0%	−36.6%
CA 39	62,048	55.4%	41.3%	3.4%	−14.1%	55.4%	39.8%	4.8%	−15.5%
CA 43	204,911	75.9%	21.4%	2.7%	−54.4%	74.2%	21.3%	4.5%	−52.9%
CA 47	140,964	67.6%	30.0%	2.4%	−37.5%	68.8%	26.6%	4.5%	−42.2%

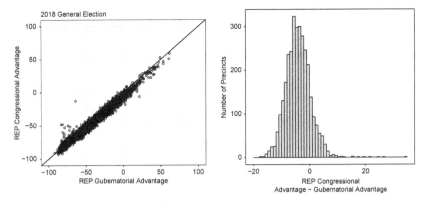

Figure 20 Republican Congressional candidates underperform Republican Governor candidate, John H. Cox, across precincts in Los Angeles County

Note: The figure on the left displays Republican Congressional advantage (*y*-axis) and Republican gubernatorial advantage (*x*-axis) by precinct. The figure on the right displays the histogram of Republican Congressional advantage minus Republican gubernatorial advantage by precinct.

4.4   What Did We Learn?

This section presented methodologies for both postelection ballot auditing and other types of forensic auditing. We showed that postelection ballot audits, whether fixed-percentage or variable-percentage, are invaluable tools for confirming the integrity of election technology and the voting process, as well as for confirming the correctness of the originally reported tabulation of the election. We also showed that using precinct-by-precinct postelection reports of turnout and votes cast, with some very simple visual analytical techniques, can provide important confirmations of an election's integrity. All of these approaches look for evidence of anomalies, outliers, or deviations from official election statistics; by showing that there are very few anomalies or deviations in the data from Orange County in 2018, we can further increase our confidence in the integrity of these important and contested elections.

Of course, many other methods can be used for anomaly or outlier detection, especially using statistical or computational modeling. Those approaches can provide further confirmation of the integrity of an election, as they can produce fewer false positives. Approaches involving sophisticated machine learning algorithms, for example, can be very useful for forensic analyses, but they require large datasets and careful attention to many different tuning parameters. Interested readers should consult Levin et al. (2016), and Zhang, Alvarez, and Levin (2019) for further details about these more advanced forensic methods.

Note that they are also not as simple to present and analyze as the visual forensics we used in this section, nor are these methods as transparent to citizens, election officials, and practitioners.

5   Auditing Voter Registration Databases

5.1   Why Monitor Voter Registration Data?

On September 22, 2017, *The New York Times* reported that the Department of Homeland Security had contacted twenty-one states, telling them that hackers had targeted their voter registration database – that voter data had not necessarily been manipulated, but that the situation was akin to "a burglar circling a house, checking for unlocked doors and windows."[35] On June 14, 2017, *Politico* reported that a former cybersecurity researcher had demonstrated the vulnerability in Georgia's handling of voter rolls, by easily breaking open access to 6.7 million voters' information which was not intended for public release, as well as the instructions and passwords required to access the central, electronic pollbook that poll workers would work with on Election Day. On May 8, 2018, the Senate Intelligence Committee ultimately concluded that, in some cases, Russian hackers had successfully penetrated voter registration databases during the 2016 election. The Committee concluded that it had "not seen any evidence that vote tallies were manipulated or that voter registration information was deleted or modified." On March 2019, the *Report on the Investigation Into Russian Interference in the 2016 Presidential Election*, commonly known as the Mueller Report, wrote that Russian intelligence had targeted private technology firms that manufactured and administered election-administrative matters such as voter registration.

Although there have been no reports of successful manipulations of voter registration databases, these accounts show that they are a target for hackers, and that they are a vulnerable aspect of American election infrastructures. In addition, there is a strong possibility that there may be internal quality issues with voter data, resulting from mistakes in data entry or from improper database management. Though most of these are unintentional, internal errors can also wreak havoc with the administration of an election.

Los Angeles County's 2018 primaries show a good example of what can happen when voter registration databases are disrupted. On Election Day, 118,509 voters were left off the rosters that were distributed to precincts, causing 2.3%

---

[35] www.nytimes.com/2017/09/22/us/politics/us-tells-21-states-that-hackers
-targeted-their-voting-systems.html; www.politico.com/magazine/story/
2017/06/14/will-the-georgia-special-election-get-hacked-215255.

of validly registered voters to resort to provisional balloting or give up on voting entirely. Contributing to confusion, strains on poll worker attention, and longer wait time, this generally caused disruptions at polling places throughout the County. The underlying reason for the error was outdated software which created empty spaces for these voters' birth dates, leading them to be classified as birth dates of zero, that is, under the voting age of 18, and ultimately left off the rolls.[36] While technically these voters' voting rights were not hampered, there was outrage on Election Day over the inconvenience of having to vote using provisional ballots. In addition, many cried foul, distrustful of the nature of the error, arguing that it could be partisan-driven or an attempt to disenfranchise voters systematically across the county or in particularly contested districts.

There were other examples in 2018. On September 5, 2018. The *Los Angeles Times* reported that with the new "motor voter" system going into effect, the Department of Motor Vehicles had incorrectly added 23,000 voters with erroneous information, such as political party preferences. On September 11, 2018, *CNN* reported that a Georgia state legislative election may have been swayed, as voters were assigned to the incorrect precincts. The same kind of mistake was also found in a Virginia House race, again enough to possibly swing the election results, according to the *Washington Post* on May 13, 2018.[37]

As we can see, there are both internal and external threats to the security and integrity of voter registration databases; considering these potential threats, the importance of ensuring accurate voter data is unquestionable. As Ansolabehere and Hersh (2014) point out, voter data serve many purposes: they assign voters to their precincts, make sure that only eligible voters can either vote in person on Election Day at each precinct or submit vote-by-mail ballots, and carry information on party registration, which is important for determining eligibility to participate in primary elections in many states. Additionally, they are passed along to political candidates and parties, who use this information in strategic persuasion and get-out-the-vote activities. Compromise of their quality can, either maliciously or inadvertently, undermine the integrity of the elections. Therefore, while the idea of auditing voter registration databases may be less

---

[36] www.lavote.net/docs/rrcc/news-releases/Final-Revised-Media-Release
-Voter-Roster.pdf?v=1.

[37] https://edition.cnn.com/2018/09/10/politics/georgia-election-ballot
-error-dan-gasaway-district-legislature-habersham-county/index.html;
www.latimes.com/politics/la-pol-ca-dmv-voter-registration-error
-20180905-story.html; www.washingtonpost.com/local/virginia-politics/
voters-assigned-to-wrong-districts-may-have-cost-democrats
-in-pivotal-virginia-race/2018/05/13/09a9dd8a-5465-11e8-a551
-5b648abe29ef_story.html.

well known than the typical "election auditing," it is another essential method of buttressing election integrity.

Ansolabehere and Hersh (2010, 2014) address the issue of voter data quality in its static state. That is, a single version of the voter data is taken at a particular point in time, and its characteristics analyzed – for example, what proportion of the data has addresses or birth dates missing. Here, we demonstrate how to evaluate voter data quality as it *changes over time*. That is, detecting which internal/external mishaps not present in yesterday's data file manifest today. Voter databases are constantly changing, so in addition to any static analysis, data quality must be assessed dynamically.

In this section, we demonstrate how to create audit data for voter registration databases using their regular *snapshots*: multiple versions of the same voter data at particular historic points in time, as also demonstrated in Kim, Schneider, and Alvarez (2019). We first establish how voter databases are shaped, as well as introduce administrative schedules surrounding their maintenance. Next, we show how we create audit data by preserving historic snapshots of the database, and linking them together using probabilistic record linkage. Afterwards, we show how the database changes over time, and how to detect anomalies in these changes. Finally, we demonstrate how useful this method would be for some hypothetical situations in which the data are disrupted via simulations. We conclude by discussing the method's utilities and future directions.

5.2   Voter Registration Databases

In Orange County, many of the specifics of voter registration database maintenance are mandated by the state-level legislation, and these regulations have changed rapidly in recent years. As of the 2018 election cycle, a voter can register to vote by three major routes: (1) they can submit a paper application to their County's elections office; (2) they can submit an online application through the statewide website (www.sos.ca.gov/elections/voter-registration/), which is an outcome of the VoteCal Project of 2015; or (3) they can be automatically enrolled while they register at the Department of Motor Vehicles (DMV) (unless they explicitly opt-out) in a newly implemented "motor voter" scheme.

The Orange County's registration record of each voter, whichever route they registered through, will contain the following information: a voter's full name, prefix, and suffix, residential and mail address, date and place of birth, political party affiliation, phone number, email address, and permanent absentee voter status. Along with these voter-entered details, the Registrar enters additional information to the voter file, such as original registration date, last registration date, last date the file was updated, precinct assignment, and the local jurisdiction to which the precinct belongs.

In Orange County, the voter registration forms ask the voter for both their California driver's license number (or a California Identification card number) and the last four digits of their Social Security Number (SSN) (Orange County Registrar of Voters, 2018). However, these fields are not provided in the files exported to our team for analysis, nor are these values strictly required to ensure the integrity of the voter registration database.

Table 7 shows a summary of the key voter-entered fields of the same May 21 snapshot. Note that unlike some other jurisdictions, such as Florida or Georgia, Orange County's database does not contain self-reported racial/ethnic identifications. However, the top ten surnames in the Orange County data are: Nguyen, Tran, Garcia, Lee, Kim, Smith, Hernandez, Le, Martinez, and Lopez. This speaks to the racial and ethnic diversity present in Orange County, including potential Vietnamese, Korean, and Hispanic surnames. In addition, note that although there is a gender field in the data, 99.7% of the entries are missing – in fact, the gender field seems to be an artifact of the new motor voter process, and was not previously mandated in other registration forms.

While we have shown the dataset summary for a particular snapshot, voter data are temporal. That is, voter data represent a dynamically changing dataset – new voters register, database administrators remove outdated voter records, and, in some cases, voter details change. All such changes are overseen by administrative clerks at the OCROV, and if validated, are entered into the system. Unless the resources at the Registrar are completely exhausted on extremely busy days, the database is changing in real-time. Data comes from the statewide registration database, paper registrations sent to the County offices, CalVoter updates from the DMV, public assistance agencies, Armed Forces recruitment offices, and other sources.

In the 2018 election cycle, from April 26, 2018 to March 2, 2020, we received 440 snapshots of the voter database, mostly snapshots from weekdays, though there are some exceptions when the Registrar's office was busy. In total, more than 60% of the date range was covered. Figure 21 shows the changes in the registration numbers by each snapshot.

There are many reasons why a voter may be added or removed or that information in their registration record might change. An added voter may be an existing citizen who has newly expressed an interest in voting, an incoming mover who has moved into the county, or young voters who have just become eligible to vote. VoteCal offers online preregistration for 16- and 17-year-olds,

Table 7 Data summary by field of May 21, 2018 snapshot

Category	Field	# of Unique Entries	# of Most Freq. Entry	Number Missing	Examples
Name	First	89,984	21,481	78	Jane
	Middle	51,609	83,035	406,428	E
	Last	188,734	26,385	0	Doe
	Name Prefix	5	466,043	488,123	Ms.
	Name Suffix	18	16,430	1,452,055	Jr.
Address	Street	786,224	93	0	100 S Grand Ave
	City	48	140,081	0	Santa Ana
	Zip Code	94	40,128	0	92705
Date of Birth		30,467	124	23	March 11, 1989
Place of Birth		319	678,187	60,999	CA
Gender		3	2,274	1,474,151	F
Political Party		46	540,859	0	No Party Preference
Contact	Phone	706,710	9,035	663,105	(714) 567-7600
	Email	452,609	382	1,018,894	jane@roc.ocgov.com

whose records will be automatically activated when they turn 18. Other existing residents or movers may register when they are doing business at the DMV, when there are successful voter registration drives, and at other locations and government agencies.

Next, there are three main reasons why a voter may be removed from the list of active voters. A voter may be found to be deceased, a voter may be an outgoing mover who has moved outside the county, or a voter may contact the Registrar and ask to cancel his or her registration. In addition, some voters may turn "inactive," and be removed from the active voter registration database.[38] These are eligible voters who simply do not receive election-related materials, due to reasons such as that on previous delivery attempts they were deemed undeliverable, and they have not voted nor have they updated/confirmed their voter registration in the last four years.

Finally, California statewide requirements mandate that re-registration is necessary when voters change their name, or change their political party preference. In Orange County, a re-registration is required when voters have "recently moved, became married, or want to change your political affiliation (party)." In addition, even if it is not a full-fledged re-registration, the voter can request to have small details changed on his or her record, such as the following:

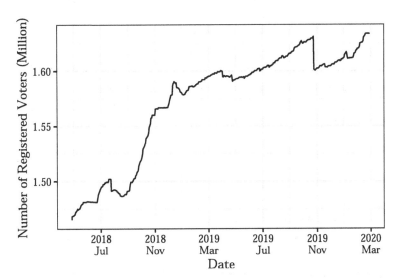

Figure 21 Daily number of Orange County voter registration records, from April 26, 2018 to March 2, 2020

---

[38] Note that in other jurisdictions, inactive voters may also be kept within the database, so to evaluate these reasons, there must be some domain expertise.

- Add/correct phone number
- Remove phone number
- Add/correct email address
- Remove email address
- Add mailing address
- Remove mailing address
- Change language preference

- Request voter notification card
- Remove permanent vote-by-mail status
- Correct name spelling
- Add or correct apartment number
- Add permanent vote-by-mail status
- Receive sample ballots by mail

In the research literature, the temporal nature of voter databases has gone largely unexplored. Voter registration databases are mostly used in political behavior research, and for many research questions, a snapshot or two of data at key instances (such as the dates of primary and general elections) suffice. In fact, the only systematic analysis of these temporal detail changes has been a technical report by Christen (2014). The authors conduct this study more for the purposes of developing computer science algorithms, as opposed to studying the integrity of voter registration data.

However, our purpose is to create audit data that can be continuously monitored for errors or foul play. For this, we need to establish stylized facts about the data-generating process and spot anomalies, if any. Naturally, the temporal nature of voter registration databases is the key source for generating the audit data, a method we explain in detail later in this section.

Note that because voter data are dynamic, duplicates emerge in the data, as in all administrative data. Table 8 shows some synthetic examples of possible duplicates. Typically, duplicates arise because they should have been merged as an update to an existing voter, but were erroneously entered as a brand new record. These "new" records are then added as separate, distinct records. Ansolabehere and Hersh (2010) estimates that one out of every sixty-five records is a duplicate in a typical voter database, that is, approximately 1.5% of the data.

5.3 Record Linkage: Finding the Same Voter

5.3.1 Record Linkage

The basic idea of monitoring voter registration databases involves quantifying changes to the database, defining the normal volume of change, and then finding anomalies. To quantify these changes to voter data – additions, deletions, and changes – for each baseline and updated snapshot, we first must determine which records in the baseline correspond to records in the updated database. This represents the basic problem of entity resolution. In Figure 22, we show a stylized relationship between baseline data and updated data, and demonstrate how records may be added, dropped, changed, or unchanged (exact matches).

Table 8 Synthetic examples of duplicates/changes in voter lists

| | Name | | | Address | | | Birth Date | Contact | |
	First	Middle	Last	Street Address	City			Phone	Email
1	Steven	B	Smith	110 S East Ave	Brea		04/26/1980	714-765-3300	N/A
2	Steven		Smith	110 S East Ave	Brea		04/26/1980	714-765-3300	smith@ex
3	Juan		Torres	200 Fig St	Irvine		02/02/1970	949-496-0601	N/A
4	Torres		Torres	200 Fig St	Irvine		02/02/1970	949-496-0601	N/A
5	Isidor		Agnes	99 6th St #72	Tustin		07/13/1960	N/A	N/A
6	Jsidor		Agne	99 6th St #72	Tustin		07/13/1960	714-205-8583	N/A
7	Anna	Clara	Zhang	203 Coast Ln	Tustin		12/01/1950	N/A	acz@ex
8	Anna	C	Zhang	101 Sunny Blvd	Brea		12/10/1950	N/A	acz@ex

Detecting and interpreting these changes demonstrates how entity resolution lies at the heart of our approach to auditing voter registration data.

Ideally, this process would be expedited by personal identifiers, such as Social Security Numbers, driver's license numbers, or an internal voter database ID designated by the state. However, given privacy concerns, real-life personal identifiers are rarely made public or available to researchers. In addition, though not the case in Orange County, there may be severe quality issues with internally assigned voter IDs, in that they may be duplicated or inaccurate. For these reasons, we decided that we would build our auditing methodology without highly sensitive identifiers. This means that we did not need to transfer and store highly sensitive personal information, and that the tools that we built could be used by other researchers, stakeholders, and election officials, who may not have access to datasets with these personal identifiers. However, not having and using these identifiers potentially makes the entity resolution process for our approach more difficult, and as we discuss in this subsection we take a number of steps to make sure that our method is as accurate as possible.

For a more general framework, in this subsection we introduce *probabilistic record linkage* (PRL), which can match records in two databases without relying on a true match status represented by some type of known ID number. Much of the technical detail is deferred to Appendix B, and this subsection is intended to give an overview of the ideas behind probabilistic linkage.

Record linkage, also called entity resolution or record matching, is identifying which records refer to the same entity across different databases – that is, real-life objects that we are interested in. In our setup, record linkage is deciding whether the voter A in one file is the same voter as voter A' in another

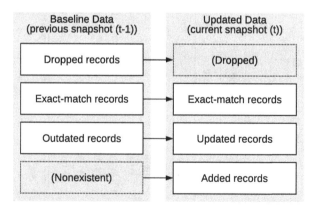

Figure 22 Comparing snapshots of temporal datasets

file. Probabilistic record linkage explicitly refers to a nondeterministic record linkage that relies on probabilistic weighting.

As a motivating demonstration, let us use examples from Table 8 and suppose that the odd rows belong to a baseline database and the even rows belong to an updated database. Deterministic matching is a rule such as the following, put in plain language similar to that of the rule-base of Hernández and Stolfo (1995):

Given two records R1 and R2,
  IF the date of birth of R1 equals the date of birth of R2,
  AND last name of R1 equals the last name of R2,
    AND first name of R1 equals the first name of R1,
    AND the address of R1 equals the address of R2,
  THEN
    R1 and R2 are the same entity.

With the above deterministic rule, only "Steven Smith" would be deemed a match between the two databases. However, if we assume that the rest of the records are also matches, the small discrepancies between them are preventing them being declared as matches by a deterministic record linkage.

5.3.2   Probabilistic Record Linkage

Probabilistic record linkage seeks to overcome this very problem – that in many databases, even when the underlying entity is the same, some entries will differ due to changes or small typos. Conceptualized by Newcombe et al. (1959), formalized by Fellegi and Sunter (1969), and extended by (Winkler (1988, 1990); Winkler & Thibaudeau, 1991), probabilistic record linkage assigns a probability to each entry pair that it will be a match, and with pairs with sufficiently high probability, will accept them as matches.

A general probabilistic record linkage framework is as follows. Between two datasets, there are common records, denoted as *matches*. Conversely, there are *nonmatches*. To paraphrase the same mathematical notations in Fellegi and Sunter (1969), we can express the idea as the following: a pair of entries from two different datasets can either belong in the (1) matched set, or the (2) unmatched set. Whether a pair of records belong to the matched or the unmatched set is a *latent variable* which determines the value of *attributes* – variables such as surnames, first names, dates of birth, and so on in our example.

If two records are a match, they are likely to have common attributes; on the other hand, if they are a nonmatch, they are less likely to do so. For example, if voter *A* is in both records, it is more likely than not that the last names of the two would agree. Conversely, if we are looking into records of two different

Framework of Probabilistic Record Linkage

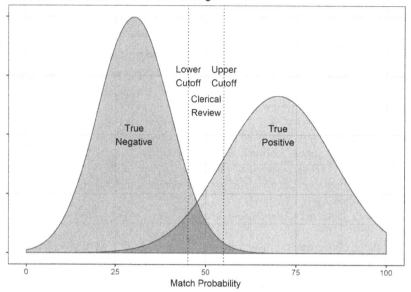

Figure 23 Probabilistic record linkage

voters *A* and *B*, their last names are more likely to disagree. Figure 23 shows this idea more clearly – that given a latent distribution, the probabilities of attribute agreements differ.

Probabilistic record linkage is ultimately a classification problem, in which each comparison vector is put either into a *matched set*, a *possibly matched set*, or an *unmatched set*, based on the level of attribute agreements. There are two types of errors in record linkage. On the one hand, there are *false positives*, or Type II errors – two records were a nonmatch, but they were classified as a match. On the other hand, there are *false negatives*, or Type I errors – two records were a match, but they were classified as a nonmatch. While there is a certain tradeoff between the two, a good record linkage seeks to minimize both, and depending on the usage, a researcher may put more emphasis on minimizing one or the other.

An optimal linkage rule is one that, given a fixed rate of errors, needs minimal human intervention. For a mathematical expression of the optimal linkage rule, see a reiteration of Fellegi and Sunter (1969) in Appendix B. The idea however, is very simple – human interventions are expensive.

Much depends on the distribution of these attributes' values. If two records in Orange County have the same last name as "Nguyen," it does not necessarily mean that the two records are the same person. Because the particular surname is relatively common, it could be that this common last name is a simple coincidence – a false positive. It is less likely to be a false positive when the surname is rarer. For instance, two records of surname "Mulligan" are more likely to be a true match than two records of surname "Smith." If email addresses as well as surnames agree, the likelihood that these records are the same entity increases, because a coincidence in email addresses is very rare.

This will be reflected in the likelihood ratio, which is a ratio between conditional probabilities of attribute agreements if it is a true match or not. Under certain assumptions, it is optimal to classify as follows:

1. If the likelihood ratio is below the lower threshold, classify as a nonmatch
2. If the likelihood ratio is between the lower threshold and the higher threshold, classify as needing clerical review
3. If the likelihood ratio is above the higher threshold, classify as a match.

By assuming conditional independence, we can use the sum of each attribute's weights as a test statistic for our classification.

5.3.3 String Distance Calculations

This means that ultimately, we need to calculate the agreement–disagreement between each attribute of the records to compare, take into consideration the frequency of the attribute values, and weight the final probability that records are a true positive match.

However, as in Table 8, two records which refer to the same entity may have discrepancies due to typos – for example, "Isidor" and "Jsidor" in lines 5–6. It then makes sense to allow for a spectrum of agreement, so that the agreement between attributes does not have to be exact, and typos are allowed. Indeed, Winkler (1990) developed a major extension of the framework by showing that accounting for typographical variations in a string comparison metric leads to better matching.

How do we quantify the similarity between string values? While there are many metrics, ranging from q-gram based string comparison, longest common substring comparison, syllable alignment distance, and so on (Christen, 2012), we will introduce two of the most commonly used string comparison metrics: (1) *Levenshtein distance* (Levenshtein, 1966) and (2) *Jaro–Winkler distance* (Jaro, 1989). Both of these metrics measure edit distances in distinct ways.

Levenshtein distance is relatively straightforward. It is the minimum number of times you would have to perform single-character edits – adds, deletes, or substitutions – for two strings to agree. For instance, the Levenshtein distance between "Isidor" and "Jsidor" would simply be 1, since only the first letter "I" has to be substituted to "J." Between "C" and "Clara," the distance would be 4, since the last four letters would have to be added to "C" to create "Clara."

The Jaro–Winkler distance is slightly more complicated. It first counts the number of common characters between two strings. A character from each string is considered common if they match and the distance between them does not exceed half the length of the longer string, as opposed to the length of the shorter string (Yancey, 2005). Then the number of transpositions is calculated, that is, the number of changes required to make the characters' orders the same. The Jaro distance is a linearly weighted measure of these numbers – see the Appendix B for details.

Winkler has modified the above Jaro distance taking into account common prefixes, similar characters, and adjusting for longer strings. The technicalities involved in the Winkler adjustment are beyond the scope of this Element, but see Yancey (2005) for a good explanation of the method. Overall, there is a wide consensus that the Jaro–Winkler distance performs very well (Cohen, Ravikumar, & Fienberg, 2003; T. N. Herzog, Scheuren, & Winkler, 2010; Yancey, 2005).

5.3.4   Implementation

We have so far shown the definitions of record linkage and probabilistic record linkage from the Fellegi–Sunter framework. We have also shown the extended framework developed by Winkler, and the different string-distance metrics that can be used.[39]

We perform the actual implementation of the probabilistic record linkage with open-source software developed by Enamorado, Fifield, and Imai (2018), available in R's CRAN library as `fastLink`. Researchers demonstrate that this package has strong computational advantages, both in its performance and execution time. We use a one-to-one match with the default threshold of 0.85, which has proven to be very accurate and efficient. Note that the authors caution that optimal thresholds are highly dependent on the data and a performance assessment with labeled data that contains true match status. We have internal IDs set by the OCROV, which are imperfect but a great measure of the underlying match status. For details on the matching and the robustness check, see Kim et al. (2019).

---

[39] For more on the proof of the fundamental optimal theorem of record linkage, see Fellegi and Sunter (1969). For a general overview of the history of record linkage and recent extensions, see T. N. Herzog, Scheuren, and Winkler (2007) and Christen (2012).

5.4   Monitoring Changes

5.4.1   Setup and Assumptions

Now that we have defined and shown how we implement probabilistic record linkage for our entity resolution problem, we can start linking our daily snapshots of the voter registration database. Since we have 440 snapshots, we create 439 linkages of the snapshots, ordered by date.

Because we have near-daily snapshots of the database, we find few snapshot-to-snapshot changes, as may be expected. Most of the 1.5 million records – usually 99% or more of the records – in the data do not change day by day. In fact, unless a large set of changes have been made to the database according to the administrative maintenance schedule, a sudden spike in the database change would be a red flag that would warrant a further, detailed investigation.

Therefore, while a more accurate approach would be to use all 1.5 million records and compare string or numeric distance between them in each field, we find it just as effective to just use records that are not exactly the same between two snapshots to perform probabilistic record linkage. That is, from Figure 22, we exclude the exact-match records. Because it is computationally intensive to calculate a string agreement metric for every field and for every comparison, this greatly reduces the necessary computational resources.

If we exclude exact matches entirely, we implicitly assume that changes are independent of the underlying distribution of the attribute frequencies. To correct for the possible biases introduced by excluding exact matches, we did a robustness check by reintroducing a small random percentage of the exact-match records to mimic the population's distribution of each attribute. We find that this robust measure hardly changes the result while dramatically increasing the computational load. Therefore we exclude exact matches.

In addition, we clearly do not have to – and should not – include all sixty-two variables in the data file, as it will break the conditional independence assumption. Hence we must select variables that (1) carry meaningful information about the real-world voter and (2) are reasonably independent of each other. We find that the combination of the following five variables worked best with the Orange County registration data:

– Last name, first name
– Date of birth
– Street number, zip-code

These were initially inspired by Ansolabehere and Hersh (2017)'s *ADGN variables* and tailored to the data we have from Orange County. The ADGN

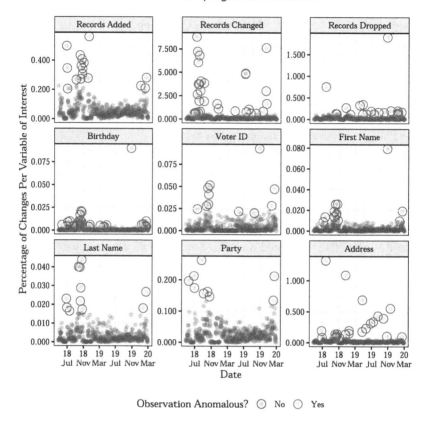

Figure 24 Anomaly detection of time-series data

variables are simply (1) address, (2) date of birth, (3) gender, and (4) name.[40] Their paper focuses on the surprising strength of exact record linkage, but again, we want to emphasize that probabilistic record linkage works better, as demonstrated in Enamorado et al. (2018). In other jurisdictions, other variables may be more appropriate, such as phone numbers and emails.

5.4.2   Adds, Deletes, and Changes

Once the matching has been performed between each consecutive snapshot, the first quantities to investigate are how many records were added, deleted, or

---

[40] Among the variables used in Ansolabehere and Hersh (2017), we do not include gender, as it is missing most of the time in our Orange County data, shown in Table 7. Although gender can be somewhat inferred using first names, voter-entered prefixes, and the few entries that actually contain self-reported gender, we find that including inferred gender on top of our selection of variables decreases performance slightly.

changed. The first row's three panels in Figure 24 show these major changes between snapshots in respective time-series. The x-axis is processing dates rather than registration/re-registration submission dates. Note that the y-axis scales of each panel differ to provide maximal information, because the number of record changes can be as large as 10% of the whole voter file, while additions or deletions do not exceed 1%.

The trends of additions, deletions, and changes are not necessarily similar. The correlation coefficient (1) between records added and records deleted is a mere 0.06, (2) between records added and records changed is 0.13, and (3) between records deleted and records changed is 0.10. This is because they reflect different underlying data-generating processes. While records added are more likely to be voter-initiated, records dropped are more likely to be administratively initiated, because few voters inform the Registrar when they move out of the jurisdiction, are no longer eligible to vote, or if any family members are recently deceased – all reasons records should be removed from active voting rolls. Therefore, the removals follow an internal maintenance schedule of the Registrar, with some governed by state or federal requirements.

Because new voter records are voluntary inputs, their trend is highly associated with salient events within the election cycle, such as each election's registration deadline, the National Voter Registration Day, Election Day, and so on.

5.4.3   Changes in Specific Fields

Of course, we might be more interested in the different types of changes taking place within the records changed. In Figure 24, we show six different panels of such changes, ranging from the time-series of records with partisan affiliation changes to name and address changes.[41]

The reason the large percentage of changes in the third panel (*Records Changed*) are not mirrored in the next two rows is because these changes were associated with internal variable recodings. One such example is a re-precincting of particular subsets of voters. Such changes are not related to substantial, real entity changes on the voter's part that the voter initiated.

Changes in the last two rows of Figure 24, other than voter IDs, are voter-initiated. Notice that changes in party affiliation and last names are similar to the trend of records added (correlation coefficient both 0.73). Others are less similar. This however hints that there is a common election dynamic

---

[41] Note that although the x-axis is the processing date, most adds/changes are reviewed and updated within the same day, or the next few days, at the latest.

that inspires new voters, as well as voters who are changing their existing information such as partisan affiliation. Table 9 shows all Pearson correlation coefficients between the nine panels in Figure 24.

5.4.4   Anomaly Detection

So far, we have descriptively investigated the trend of changes by each field, but have not defined a "normal" volume of change. The adds, deletes, and changes are clearly not uniformly distributed. They also do not have a clear seasonality. Rather, it is a complex function of election dynamics and the activities of the entities involved in voter registration.

While there can be many different ways to define normal and abnormal volumes of changes in this setting, here we demonstrate the simplest outlier detection approach, using the interquartile range (IQR). The IQR method takes a series of data and calculates the first and the third quartiles ($Q1$ and $Q3$). It then calculates the IQR, which is their difference: $IQR = Q3 - Q1$. Given an IQR factor x, it then calculates the following range:

$$[Q1 - x \times IQR, Q3 + x \times IQR] \tag{5.1}$$

and deems the data outside this range as outliers. The usual choice for x is either 1.5 or 3, depending on whether it is moderate or extreme outlier detection. Our choice is the latter. Prior to applying the IQR, we perform seasonal decomposition and detrending by LOESS smoother via R package `anomalize`.[42] In addition, we regress out the effects of the day of the week, the gap between snapshots in terms of the number of days. This is to account for the fact that (1) daily snapshots are not provided on the weekends, and (2) there are periods of missing data when the Registrar was busy. We also net out the effects of month and year.[43]

In Figure 24, we show the outliers detected by the IQR method as *circled red dots*. While the number of them may at first seem surprising, when individually investigated, these all turned out to be the result of normal maintenance activities, or as expected key election-related deadlines. For instance, party affiliation's first flagged date is May 21, which was the primary election's registration deadline. The flagged dates for records dropped were National Change of Address (NCOA) processing dates. Each time the data we received was

---

[42] We could also detrend by piecewise medians as employed in some commercial applications such as Twitter (Vallis, Hochenbaum, & Kejariwal, 2014), but as suggested by the package itself, this detrending seems more fit for the low-growth, high-seasonality data.

[43] While variables have been pooled for regression in Kim et al. (2019) to account for the number of snapshots, which were only 252 at the time, now the variables are treated separately as there are almost twice the snapshots, spanning more than two years.

Table 9 Correlation between changes to the database

	Added	Changed	Dropped	Birthday	Voter ID	First Name	Last Name	Party	Address
Added	1.00	0.13	0.06	0.27	0.41	0.42	0.73	0.73	0.12
Changed	0.13	1.00	0.10	0.07	0.10	0.11	0.12	0.11	0.18
Dropped	0.06	0.10	1.00	0.83	0.55	0.73	0.18	0.18	0.42
Birthday	0.27	0.07	0.83	1.00	0.80	0.95	0.48	0.36	0.10
Voter ID	0.41	0.10	0.55	0.80	1.00	0.91	0.77	0.52	0.12
First Name	0.42	0.11	0.73	0.95	0.91	1.00	0.68	0.52	0.12
Last Name	0.73	0.12	0.18	0.48	0.77	0.68	1.00	0.73	0.15
Party	0.73	0.11	0.18	0.36	0.52	0.52	0.73	1.00	0.13
Address	0.12	0.18	0.42	0.10	0.12	0.12	0.15	0.13	1.00

updated, we delivered a report to the OCROV, and each "anomaly" was manually determined to be an intentional maintenance or a normal peak in voters' activities.

One particular point that stands out from Figure 24 is that there are sudden spikes in changes in the address. This may seem peculiar, and it did initially raise concerns when the initial monitoring report was delivered to the Registrar. However, it turned out that this is the result of regular maintenance activities, namely NCOA processing. California is mandated by the Help America Vote Act of 2002 (HAVA) to utilize the NCOA service provided by the United States Postal Service (USPS) in order to find out whether the existing, active voters have moved and (1) need sample ballots sent to a new address, or (2) are no longer eligible to vote because they have moved out of county. A batch processing can result in a sudden spike in changes in the address.

Again, we want to emphasize that while we did not find any particular problems in OCROV's data, this method can identify clear administrative issues, such as the large-scale removal of records. And while we have shown this with data gathered from 2018 to 2020, if more data are accumulated for a longer period of time, it can serve as a baseline for anomaly detection in future election cycles. With more data, we can start venturing into more sophisticated anomaly detection mechanisms as well, such as building a full model of administrative changes in voter data and finding deviations from predicted values.

5.5   Anomaly Detection: Simulations

While we find no particular spikes that seem to indicate major issues for the Orange County data, it is useful to demonstrate what anomalies we could potentially detect via simulations. In this subsection, we intentionally manipulate the voter data to imitate internal or external disruptions.

We will simulate the aforementioned Los Angeles 2018 primary example, in which 2.3% of the date of births were changed. Figure 25 shows the result, where July 11, 2019's changes were changed to match the change rate in the real-life example. Only the "Birthday" panel should change, as we have not changed any data in other variables' time-series.

The simulated change is immediately detected with the given anomaly detection tools. Given that birthdays rarely change in a voter registration database, this is especially prominent, compared to Figure 24. Note that this has changed the previously detected small spikes in birthdays which are, in most cases, no longer deemed anomalies, as the distribution of changes in birthdays has shifted slightly.

Note that this relies on the amount of data accumulated, which can inform us that the simulated 2.3% change in birthdays is at odds with what we expect from the data. The anomaly detection is only meaningful if we have substantial knowledge about the data-generating process – which makes it all the more important to keep a record of what happens periodically.

5.6   What Did We Learn?

In this section, we argued that there are many potential threats to the integrity of the voter registration database, both from internal and external sources. While most of them are unintentional, we would like to detect and possibly deter them by checking the data as it changes over time. Hence we demonstrated how to create audit data from periodic snapshots of the voter registration database. This helps us monitor the quality of the data dynamically.

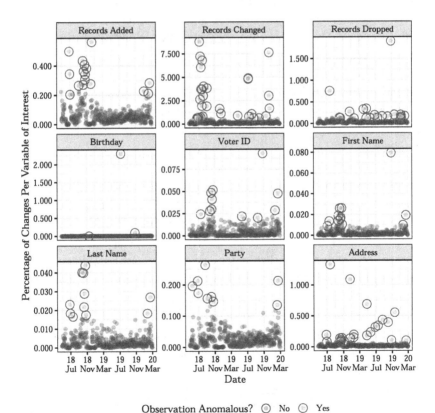

Figure 25 Anomaly detection with simulated changes

We first observed the data-generating process of voter registration – what the Orange County voter registration database contains, and how it is updated. We then illustrated how to link voter rolls of two different time periods, and have given a detailed overview of probabilistic record linkage. Finally, we show the time-series of records added, dropped, or changed when record linkage is applied to the OCROV data, and apply the IQR method for anomaly detection.

We demonstrated how we were able to detect large changes to the databases that seem anomalous, and have cross-checked all detected instances with the Registrar of Voters. While a couple of data points raised red flags for both our team and the Registrar, upon retrospective investigation, the Registrar found that they had performed administrative maintenance on those dates such as NCOA processing, and that nothing was out of the ordinary. Once we recognized these internal patterns, we could better validate incoming data and more accurately evaluate the patterns in the time-series of changes. In addition, via simulations, we have shown that we would have been able to detect the accidental changes to dates of birth in Los Angeles, 2018.

All in all, the method provides a strong check against possible mishaps with voter data. The Registrar was very interested in and satisfied with our final product, and we continue to monitor their voter data. As more election cycles come and go, the baseline data will accumulate and the prior on the data-generating process strengthen. We are working on a more principled, model-based statistical anomaly detection to improve upon the IQR method, and the code for data matching and change extractions are in a public GitHub repository.

We hope other jurisdictions will begin to adopt this methodology. This will provide strong assurances that there is nothing out of the ordinary with changes to voter data, heightening the public's trust in the integrity of the voter registration data in jurisdictions using this methodology.

Again, to make this possible, several things must be emphasized. First, we must preserve periodic snapshots of the data, or at the very least all transaction logs pertaining to the changes to the data. Second, the data must be sufficiently accumulated to provide a strong prior over what are the normal volumes of change. Third, domain expertise on a particular database and frequent, transparent communication with election officials will help guide us toward more principled anomaly detection. We do recognize that the first two are not easy for smaller, resource-capped jurisdictions. However, we recommend that some resources be allocated to preserving those historic datasets.

The previously discussed 2018 Senate report recommends that state and local officials "undertake intensive security audits of state and local voter registration systems, ideally utilizing an outside entity." Indeed, in 2018, many states and counties scrambled to have external auditors review their voter registration systems and other components of the election administration. The Department of Homeland Security (DHS) has provided security audits for many jurisdictions, and we believe that SQL injections and other attacks on voter registration data could be better deterred. We believe our method can serve as a complementary tool to monitor the integrity of the voter registration database, especially when unwanted changes take place internally – either as a result of simple, innocent mistakes or due to undetected manipulation.

6   Evaluating Election Integrity
6.1   What Have We Learned?

Each section in this Element presents important substantive and methodological contributions. Here, we quickly summarize these contributions, and then discuss how they all come together to allow for a summary evaluation of election integrity.

On the substantive side, we have presented considerable evidence that indicates that in 2018, the primary and general elections in Orange County, California, were administered freely and fairly. We examined a number of different sources and types of data, each giving us important evaluative information about different aspects of the election's administration and technology. First, we monitored the election using data collected from Twitter – and found very little indication in those data that voters, the public, stakeholders, and the parties and candidates who contested the election, reported major problems or issues with the election process in Orange County.

Next, we examined data from a large-scale survey of registered voters in Orange County, conducted immediately after the November general election. These surveys gave voters an opportunity to report back to us if they had any problems when they tried to register, to obtain, to mark, and to return their ballot. We also asked them a large number of questions about their confidence in the administration of these elections, and for their opinions about election fraud. Overall, the postelection survey indicated that Orange County voters were satisfied with the service they received when they tried to vote, reporting very few problems with the process and voting technology. Overall, they appeared very confident in the integrity of elections in Orange County.

Then, we looked at various statistical forensics (focusing our attention in this section on the November general election). These forensics looked for anomalies in precinct-level turnout, and in precinct-by-precinct candidate vote shares. In this section we examined the precinct-level Statement of Votes data, and we did not find any evidence of anomalies that had the potential to influence the outcome of the election. We also audited the postelection ballot audits that the Registrar conducted following the November general election, and reported that those audits show that the election technologies worked as expected and that the original tabulations of (selected) elections produced the correct outcome.

Finally, we audited in detail the most important administrative database used for this election, the voter registration database, for evidence of administrative error or potentially malicious activity. As we discussed in that section, using our original and novel approach to voter registration database auditing, we find no evidence of external manipulations or internal aberrations that harm the integrity of the voter registration database. Instead, we determine that all changes to this highly dynamic dataset during the 2018 election cycle were the result of traceable administrative changes to the data.

This all leads to an important ecological conclusion – that these elections were conducted with integrity, and that voters and stakeholders should feel confident that they were administered freely and fairly. In each dimension of the election administration process, and with the various types of data that we collected and analyzed, we observe evidence of election integrity.

On the methodological side, we present here a number of advances in the study of election performance and election auditing. In the past, most election performance studies have been limited largely to costly and inefficient mechanisms for determining the integrity of an election – in-person election observation, voter experience surveys, and postelection ballot audits. We do not criticize the usefulness of these methods for studying election performance, and in fact incorporate many of these techniques into our methodology.

Rather, we add to the existing literature a number of election performance methodologies that serve to provide further data on election integrity, many of which are less costly to implement, and can be conducted in near real-time. As an example, social media monitoring and voter registration database auditing are both new methods that, in association with the types of methods used in previous studies, can help to further buttress and improve the evaluation of the performance of an election.

6.2 The Future of Election Performance Monitoring

Election integrity and security is an important concern, and as we argued in this Element, there is a growing need for thorough and independent monitoring of election administration and technology. Our goal has been to try to build tools that allow us to evaluate the integrity of an election and that involve minimal assistance from those running elections. Ideally, we could build methodologies that only use passive and real-time monitoring and no direct involvement on the part of election officials. Thus, as we look ahead to future election cycles, we will continue to develop these (and other) election performance methodologies that can be used in a similar holistic manner in order to gauge the integrity of elections. This is not to say that election officials are not trustworthy – rather, that by providing an independent perspective on the quality of the administration of an election, independent and transparent analyses can give both the public and administrators valuable feedback about election integrity.

An important issue, however, is scale. In our 2018 project, we focused on a single county. Admittedly, Orange County is a relatively large election jurisdiction, and is quite diverse, with a long and complicated ballot. We are confident that these methods can be deployed readily in jurisdictions of this size and scope in the future. But the question remains: how can we use these methods in jurisdictions that are significantly larger? The good news is that some of our methods, like social media monitoring, will actually work better as we focus our analysis on larger jurisdictions (say Los Angeles County, the State of California, the West Coast, or at some point, perhaps the entire United States). On the other hand, some of our methods (like voter registration monitoring) are computationally intensive at present, so we will need to work to make these methods more efficient, and to explore how to utilize larger-scale computational facilities to implement them in real-time. Making sure that these techniques can scale will be an important priority for our research team in the near future.

A second issue is how we aggregate election performance across different analyses or performance dimensions in each jurisdiction, so that we can compare across jurisdictions and produce a summary statistic that might indicate whether one election has more integrity than another. This could be done in a single jurisdiction across time, across multiple jurisdictions in a single election cycle, or over multiple jurisdictions across different election cycles. This is a complicated question, as there is no easy way to produce simple summary statistics like these, despite efforts by other scholars, for example Gerken (2009).

While this question is going to be the subject of future work for our research group, we have some guidance for other scholars and policymakers. It is possible to produce outcome metrics from the different performance tools, such as the percentage of registered voters expressing confidence in the election, the percentages of social media posts reporting positive experiences, and so on. Those metrics could then be weighted, and aggregated into a composite score that could be used in comparative evaluations. One question is how to weight different performance metrics, which is an important issue – they could be weighted equally, or weighted in terms of their importance for a particular evaluation study. But whichever weighting scheme is used, the researcher needs to be transparent about the weighting of different evaluation factors, and to justify the assumptions behind the weighting decisions.

Another lingering question is whether these methodologies will perform well outside of the United States. We believe the answer is yes; that quantitative and data-driven election monitoring and auditing will work in other nations. The issue is that as we look to apply this rubric to those other nations, the specifics of what we audit, how we audit, and what data we analyze will naturally change. There have been efforts to study voter confidence and satisfaction with the voting experience outside the United States, and those studies provide a great deal of useful insight into how researchers might design comprehensive analyses of voter experiences outside of the American context (Alvarez, Katz, & Pomares, 2011). There have been many studies using statistical forensics to analyze electoral turnout and candidate vote-share data (see Levin et al., 2016; Zhang et al., 2019, for a review of many of the recent papers). Furthermore, using social media to monitor elections and political behavior outside of the United States has also been the focus of recent research (Klasnja et al., 2018). To the best of our knowledge, there have not been academic efforts to quantitatively evaluate the integrity or accuracy of voter registration data (in nations that require voter registration) or other lists of voting-eligible citizens (in nations that do not require voter registration). But the bottom line is that the methods discussed in this Element can, and should, be used to determine the integrity of democratic elections outside the United States.

Finally, to the extent that we, as social scientists and methodologists, are concerned about making the results of our work on election security and integrity usable and meaningful outside of academia, we need to pay close attention to transparency – making our work accessible to nonscientists, and working to produce analyses in a timely and open fashion. In some ways, these goals are antithetical to science; as scientists, we typically are concerned with communicating to other scientists, and often are not concerned about reporting the results of our studies rapidly (on the order of days or weeks). Thus, one important set of lessons we learned in this project was to focus on analytical methods that can be reported rapidly, and that we can clearly communicate to election officials and the public.

Appendix A

Appendix to Section 3: Voter and Poll Worker Surveys

A1 Survey Weighting via Raking

The primary way that survey researchers deal with the discrepancy between the characteristics of the survey sample and the target population of interest is a procedure known as calibration weighting (Deville & Sarndal, 1992). To do so, let x_{ic} denote whether respondent i possesses characteristic c and let t_c denote the total number of individuals of target population with characteristic c. For instance, x_{ic} may be an indicator for respondent i registered with no party preference and t_c would be the number of Orange County registered voters indicating no party preference during registration.

A commonly used calibration weighting procedure, known as raking, seeks to find a set of weights $(w_1, \ldots, w_n)$, one for each respondent, that minimize $\sum_i w_i \log(w_i)$ subject to the constraint that $t_c = \sum_i w_i x_{ic}$ for characteristic $c = 1, \ldots, C$ (Särndal & Lundström, 2005). In words, raking (or any other calibration weighting procedure) aims to ensure the weighted sample matches the target population in terms of the prespecified characteristics by imposing minimal up- or down-weighting of individual responses. Intuitively, since permanent absentee voters are overrepresented in our sample, to get estimates representative for registered voters in Orange County as a whole, we impose minimal down-weighting so that the weighted sample has the same fraction of permanent absentee voters as the population.

A2 Structural Topic Models for Open-Ended Survey Responses

To analyze open-ended questions, we adopt the structural topic model (Roberts et al., 2014), which is based on a classical generative model of text known as the latent Dirichlet allocation (Blei et al., 2003). The classical model posits that, for each survey response d, a multinomial distribution over "topics" θ_d is drawn from a global Dirichlet distribution Dirichlet(α). Then for each word $w_{d,n}$ in response d, a topic $z_{d,n}$ is drawn from the multinomial distribution Mult(θ_d). Finally the word $w_{d,n}$ itself is drawn from a topic-specific multinomial distribution Mult$(\beta_{z_{d,n}})$. Intuitively, a survey response may be about two topics: (1)

the problem of not receiving mail ballots and (2) the problem of a voter's name not appearing on the roster, with each topic corresponding to words associated with the topic and their frequencies of occurrence. For example, the topic of not receiving mail ballots may be represented by a distribution of words concentrated on "ballots," "receive," "mail," "never," and "arrive." A structural topic model further parametrized the global distribution and the topic-specific multinomial distributions using respondent characteristics.

Appendix B

Appendix to Section 5: Auditing Voter Registration Databases

This Appendix contains the mathematical details for Section 5. Some of the text is repetitive.

Mathematically, the idea of record linkage is expressed as follows: for a pair of records (a, b), there exists a *comparison vector* of K attributes, where each γ^k for $k = 1, \cdots, K$ indicates such statements as "the last name between records a and b agrees" or "the date of birth between records a and b disagrees."

$$\gamma[a, b] = [\gamma^1(a, b), \cdots, \gamma^K(a, b)] \tag{B-1}$$

A linkage rule L determines whether each comparison vector belongs to A_1 (matched set), A_2 (possibly matched set), or A_3 (unmatched set). That is, the linkage rule allows for uncertainty in the form of A_2, which usually requires human attention, or *clerical review*. Record linkage is hence a classification problem of comparing records and classifying them into A_1, A_2, or A_3.

There are two types of errors in record linkage. On the one hand, there are *false positives*, or Type II errors, which can be denoted as $\Pr[A_1|U]$; i.e., two records were a nonmatch, but they were classified as a match. On the other hand, there are *false negatives*, or Type I errors, which can be denoted as $\Pr[A_3|M]$; i.e., two records were a match, but they were classified as a nonmatch.

Denote the level of these errors as respectively μ and λ. Given a set of all comparisons Γ and the errors, the linkage rule $L(\mu, \lambda, \Gamma)$ is optimal if

$$\Pr[A_2|L] \leq \Pr[A_2|L'] \tag{B-2}$$

for any other linkage rule L'. This can be interpreted as requiring minimal human intervention given the admissible error levels, as human intervention is expensive. As Fellegi and Sunter (1969) write,

This seems a reasonable approach since in applications the decision $\Pr[A_2]$ will require expensive manual linkage operations; alternatively, if the probability of $\Pr[A_2]$ is not small, the linkage process is of doubtful utility.

Now suppose there is a comparison vector γ_j on records a and b. For each field $k = 1, \cdots, K$, define the conditional probabilities of γ_j^k given M or U:

$$
\begin{aligned}
m_j^k(\gamma_j) &= \Pr[\gamma_j^k(a, b) | (a, b) \in M] \\
u_j^k(\gamma_j) &= \Pr[\gamma_j^k(a, b) | (a, b) \in U]
\end{aligned}
\tag{B-3}
$$

The conditional probabilities of γ_j are simply denoted as $m(\gamma_j)$ and $u(\gamma_j)$. We then define a likelihood ratio, also denoted as odds ratio or agreement ratio:

$$
R[\gamma_j(a, b)] = m(\gamma_j)/u(\gamma_j)
\tag{B-4}
$$

Note that the distribution of these attributes' values matter. If two records in Orange County have the same last name as "Nguyen," it does not necessarily mean that the two records are the same person. Because the particular surname is relatively common, it could be that this common last name is a simple coincidence. That is, linking these records would be a false positive. It is less likely to be a false positive when the surname is rarer – two records of surname "Mulligan" are more likely to be a true match than two records of surname "Smith." If email addresses as well as surnames agree, the likelihood that these records are the same entity increases, because a coincidence in email addresses are very rare. This will be reflected in the likelihood ratio.

Let us order comparison vectors γ_j for $j = 1, \cdots, J$ by the likelihood ratio, and choose upper and lower cutoff values of the ratio, respectively denoted as T_μ and T_λ. Under certain assumptions, the linkage rule is optimal if the decision rule is as follows, given a fixed level of μ and λ:

– Records with $R[\gamma_j(a, b)] \leq T_\lambda$ are classified as nonmatches
– Records with $T_\lambda < R[\gamma_j(a, b)] < T_\mu$ are classified as potential matches that require clerical review
– Records with $T_\mu \leq R[\gamma_j(a, b)]$ are classified as matches

If we assume that γ^k for $k = 1, \cdots, K$ are conditionally independent distributed, the calculations for record linkage are greatly simplified. That is, if the two records are nonmatches, a coincidence that their last names are the same are independent of the probability that their addresses will be coincidentally the same. Vice versa, if the two records are matches, the probability that the addresses will not agree is independent of the probability that the last name will be different. Discussions of relaxing the conditional independence assumption can be found in Enamorado, Fifield, and Imai (2018).

In this case, for $\gamma[a, b] = [\gamma^1(a, b), \cdots, \gamma^K(a, b)]$, the following holds:

$$m(\gamma_j) = \prod_{k=1}^{K} \Pr[\gamma^k | M] = \prod_{k=1}^{K} m(\gamma_j^k)$$

$$u(\gamma_j) = \prod_{k=1}^{K} \Pr[\gamma^k | U] = \prod_{k-1}^{K} u(\gamma_j^k)$$

(B-5)

Each $m(\gamma_j^k)$ and $u(\gamma_j^k)$, which are our parameters of estimation, can be used to compute the *individual comparison weights* for each attribute k, which is simply a log of the likelihood ratio:

$$w^k(\gamma_j^k) = \log(m(\gamma_j^k)) - \log(u(\gamma_j^k))$$

(B-6)

The sum of the weight of each attribute can be used as a test statistic, namely the *total comparison weight* (Winkler, 1988):

$$w(\gamma_j) = \sum_{k=1}^{K} w^k(\gamma_j^k)$$

(B-7)

That is, Figure 23's y-axis is really the sum of each attribute weights.

To compute our parameters, the following likelihood function is used: given $j = 1, \cdots, J$ of available record pairs to compare,

$$\begin{aligned} L &= \prod_{j=1}^{J} \Pr(\gamma_j) \\ &= \prod_{j=1}^{J} (m(\gamma_j) \cdot \Pr(M) + u(\gamma_j) \cdot \Pr(U)) \end{aligned}$$

(B-8)

Given the data, we can now calculate the maximum likelihood. Usually, this is performed by the Expectation-Maximization (EM) algorithm. For details on the EM algorithm, we defer to T. N. Herzog, Scheuren, and Winkler (2007) whose Chapter 9 provides an excellent overview of the algorithm.

As demonstrated, we need to calculate the agreement–disagreement between each attribute of the records to compare, take into consideration the frequency of the attribute values, and weight the final probability that records are a true positive match. However, as in Table 8, two records which refer to the same entity may have some discrepancies due to a typo – for example, "Isidor" and "Jsidor" in lines 5–6. It then makes sense to allow for a spectrum of agreement, so that the agreement between attributes does not have to be exact, and typos are allowed. Indeed, a major extension of the framework was developed by Winkler (1990), who showed that using a string comparison metric that accounts for typographical variations leads to better matching.

How do we quantify the similarity between string values? While there are many metrics ranging from q-gram-based string comparison, longest common substring comparison, syllable alignment distance, and so on (Christen, 2012), we will introduce two of the most commonly used string comparison metrics, which are (1) *Levenshtein distance* (Levenshtein, 1966), and (2) *Jaro Winkler distance* (Jaro, 1989), both measuring edit distances in distinct ways.

Levenshtein distance is relatively straightforward. It is the minimum number of times you would have to perform single-character edits – adds, deletes, or substitutions – for two strings to agree. For instance, the Levenshtein distance between "Isidor" and "Jsidor" would simply be 1, since only the first letter "I" has to be substituted to "J." Between "C" and "Clara," the distance would be 4, since the last four letters would have to be added to "C" to create "Clara."

The Jaro–Winkler distance is slightly more complicated. It first counts the number of common characters between two strings and the number of transpositions of these common characters. A character from each string is considered common if they match and the distance between them does not exceed half the length of the longer string n, as opposed to the length of the shorter string m (Yancey, 2005). The total number of these common characters can be denoted by c. Then the number of transpositions t is calculated, i.e., whether the characters' orders are the same or not between the strings.

$$\text{sim}_{Jaro} = \frac{1}{3} \cdot \left(\frac{c}{m} + \frac{c}{n} + \frac{c-t}{c} \right) \tag{B-9}$$

Winkler has modified the above Jaro distance taking into account common prefixes, similar characters, and adjusting for longer strings. The technicalities involved in the Winkler adjustment are out of the scope of this Element, but are very well explained in Yancey (2005). The overall consensus is that the Jaro–Winkler distance performs very well Cohen, Ravikumar, & Fienberg, 2003; T. N. Herzog, Scheuren, & Winkler, 2010; Yancey, 2005.

We have so far shown the definitions of record linkage and probabilistic record linkage from the Fellegi–Sunter framework. We have also shown the extended framework developed by Winkler, and the different string-distance metrics that can be used. For more on the proof of the fundamental optimal theorem of record linkage, see Fellegi and Sunter (1969). For a generic overview of the history of record linkage and recent extensions, see T. N. Herzog et al. (2007) and Christen (2012).

The actual implementation of the probabilistic record linkage is performed by an open-source software developed by Enamorado et al. (2018), available in R's CRAN library `fastLink`. The package has been shown to have strong computational advantages, both in its performance and execution time, as demonstrated in the paper. We use a one-to-one match with the default threshold of 0.85, which has proven to be very accurate and efficient. Note that the authors caution that optimal thresholds are highly dependent on the data and a performance assessment with labeled data that contains true match status. We have internal IDs set by the OCROV, which are imperfect but a good measure of the underlying match status – i.e., whether the two records belong to set M or U.

References

Adams-Cohen, N. J., Hao, C., Jia, C., Matschke, N., & Alvarez, R. M. (2017). *Election monitoring using Twitter* (Working Paper No. 129). California Institute of Technology. Retrieved from `http://vote.caltech.edu/working-papers/129`

Alvarez, R. M., Atkeson, L. R., & Hall, T. E. (2012a). *Confirming elections: Creating confidence and integrity through election auditing.* Palgrave Macmillan.

Alvarez, R. M., Atkeson, L. R., & Hall, T. E. (2012b). *Evaluating elections: A handbook of methods and standards.* Cambridge University Press. doi: http://dx.doi.org/10.1017/CBO9781139226547

Alvarez, R. M., Atkeson, L. R., Levin, I., & Li, Y. (2019). Paying attention to inattentive survey respondents. *Political Analysis, 27*(2), 145–162. doi: 10.1017/pan.2018.57

Alvarez, R. M., Cao, J., and Li, Y. (2020). *Voter experiences, perceptions of fraud, and voter confidence* (Working Paper No. 139). Caltech/MIT Voting Technology Project. Retrieved from `http://vote.caltech.edu/working-papers/139`.

Alvarez, R. M., & Hall, T. E. (2006). Controlling democracy: The principal–agent problems in election administration. *Policy Studies Journal, 34*(4), 491–510. doi: 10.1111/j.1541-0072.2006.00188.x

Alvarez, R. M., Hall, T. E., and Llewellyn, M. H. (2008). Are Americans confident their ballots are counted? *The Journal of Politics* 70(3), 754–766.

Alvarez, R. M., Katz, G., & Pomares, J. (2011). The impact of new technologies on voter confidence in Latin America: Evidence from e-voting experiments in Argentina and Colombia. *Journal of Information Technology & Politics, 8*(2), 199–217.

Alvarez, R. M., & Katz, J. N. (2008). The case of the 2002 general election. In R. M. Alvarez, T. E. Hall, & S. D. Hyde (Eds.), *Election fraud: Detecting and deterring electoral manipulation* (pp. 149–162). Brookings Institution Press.

Alvarez, R. M., Katz, J. N., Hill, S. A., & Hartman, E. K. (2012). Machines versus humans: The counting and recounting of prescored punchcard ballots. In R. M. Alvarez, L. R. Atkeson, & T. E. Hall (Eds.), *Confirming elections: Creating confidence and integrity through election auditing* (pp. 73–88). Palgrave Macmillan.

Alvarez, R. M., & Schousen, M. M. (1993). Policy moderation or conflicting expectations: Testing the international models of split-ticket voting. *American Politics Quarterly, 21*(4), 410–438.

Ansolabehere, S., & Hersh, E. (2010). The quality of voter registration records: A state-by-state analysis. *Report, Caltech/MIT Voting Technology Project.* http://www.vote.caltech.edu/reports/6

Ansolabehere, S., & Hersh, E. (2014). Voter registration: The process and quality of lists. In Barry C. Burden and Charles Stewart III (Eds.), *The measure of American elections* (pp. 61–90). Cambridge University Press. https://books.google.com/books?hl=en&lr=&id=mTADBAAAQBAJ&oi=fnd&pg=PR13&dq=the+measure+of+american+elections&ots=Fo-4IxJi5-&sig=mr-EoL99n3vESByjQCzsRo9rPv8#v=onepage&q=the%20measure%20of%20american%20elections&f=false

Ansolabehere, S., & Hersh, E. (2017). ADGN: An algorithm for record linkage using address, date of birth, gender, and name. *Statistics and Public Policy, 4*(1), 1–10.

Atkeson, L. R., Alvarez, R. M., & Hall, T. E. (2015). Voter confidence: How to measure it and how it differs from government support. *Election Law Journal: Rules, Politics, and Policy, 14*(3), 207–219. doi: 10.1089/elj.2014.0293

Atkeson, L. R., & Saunders, K. L. (2007). The effect of election administration on voter confidence: A local matter? *PS: Political Science and Politics, 40*(4), 655–660. Retrieved from www.jstor.org/stable/20452045.

Barberá, P. (2015). Birds of the same feather tweet together: Bayesian ideal point estimation using Twitter data. *Political Analysis, 23*(1), 76–91.

Beauchamp, N. (2017). Predicting and interpolating state-level polls using Twitter textual data. *American Journal of Political Science, 61*(2), 490–503.

Beber, B., & Scacco, A. (2012). What the numbers say: A digit-based test for election fraud. *Political Analysis, 20*(2), 211–234.

Benoit, K., & Nulty, P. (2016). *quanteda: Quantitative analysis of textual data* [Computer software manual]. Retrieved from http://github.com/kbenoit/quanteda (R package version 0.9.1–11)

Berinsky, A. J., Margolis, M. F., & Sances, M. W. (2014). Separating the shirkers from the workers? Making sure respondents pay attention on self-administered surveys. *American Journal of Political Science, 58*(3), 739–753. doi: 10.1111/ajps.12081

Bessi, A., & Ferrara, E. (2016). Social bots distort the 2016 US presidential election online discussion. *First Monday, 21*(11).

Blei, D. M., Ng, A. Y., & Jordan, M. I. (2003). Latent Dirichlet allocation. *Journal of Machine Learning Research, 3*(Jan.), 993–1022.

Breuninger, K. (2018, November). Missing power cords, foreclosures: Here's where voters are running into problems at the polls. *CNBC*. Retrieved from www.cnbc.com/2018/11/06/heres-where-voters-are-running-into-problems-at-the-polls.html

Burden, B. C., & Kimball, D. C. (2002). *Why Americans split their tickets: Campaigns, competition, and divided government*. University of Michigan Press.

Burnap, P., Gibson, R., Sloan, L., Southern, R., & Williams, M. (2016). 140 characters to victory? Using Twitter to predict the UK 2015 general election. *Electoral Studies, 41*, 230–233.

Campbell, A., Converse, P., Miller, W., & Stokes, D. (1980). *The American Voter*. University of Chicago Press.

Cantú, F., & Saiegh, S. M. (2011). Fraudulent democracy? An analysis of Argentina's infamous decade using supervised machine learning. *Political Analysis, 19*(4), 409–433.

Ceron, A., Curini, L., & Iacus, S. M. (2015). Using sentiment analysis to monitor electoral campaigns: Method matters – evidence from the United States and Italy. *Social Science Computer Review, 33*(1), 3–20.

Chandola, V., Banerjee, A., & Kumar, V. (2009). Anomaly detection: A survey. *ACM Computing Surveys (CSUR), 41*(3), 15.

Christen, P. (2012). *Data matching: Concepts and techniques for record linkage, entity resolution, and duplicate detection*. Springer Science & Business Media.

Christen, P. (2014). *Preparation of a real temporal voter data set for record linkage and duplicate detection research* (Tech. Rep.). The Australian National University. Retrieved from http://users.cecs.anu.edu.au/~Peter.Christen/publications/ncvoter-report-29june2014.pdf

Cohen, W., Ravikumar, P., & Fienberg, S. (2003). A comparison of string metrics for matching names and records. In *Proceedings of the KDD-2003 Workshop on Data Cleaning, Record Linkage, and Object Consolidation* Washington, DC, August, 2003 (Vol. 3, pp. 73–78).

Conover, M. D., Ratkiewicz, J., Francisco, M., Goncalves, B., Menczer, F., & Flammini, A. (2011). Political polarization on Twitter. In *Proceedings of the 5th international conference on weblogs and social media*. Barcelona, Spain: AAAI.

Deville, J.-C., & Sarndal, C.-E. (1992). Calibration estimators in survey sampling. *Journal of the American Statistical Association, 87*(418), 376–382. Retrieved from www.jstor.org/stable/2290268 doi: 10.2307/2290268

Dreyfuss, E. (2018, November). Georgia voting machine issues heighten scrutiny on Brian Kemp. *Wired.*

Enamorado, T., Fifield, B., & Imai, K. (2018). Using a probabilistic model to assist merging of large-scale administrative records. *American Political Science Review*, 1–19.

Epstein, R. J. (2018, August 22). Republican Troy Balderson declared winner in tight Ohio special election. *The Wall Street Journal.*

Fellegi, I. P., & Sunter, A. B. (1969). A theory for record linkage. *Journal of the American Statistical Association, 64*(328), 1183–1210.

Ferrara, E. (2017). Disinformation and social bot operations in the run up to the 2017 French presidential election. *CoRR, abs/1707.00086*. Retrieved from http://arxiv.org/abs/1707.00086

Gerken, H. (2009). *The democracy index: Why our election system is failing and how to fix it*. Princeton University Press.

Golbeck, J., Grimes, J. M., & Rogers, A. (2010). Twitter use by the US Congress. *Journal of the American Society for Information Science and Technology, 61*(8), 1612–1621.

Graham, T., Jackson, D., & Broersma, M. (2016). New platform, old habits? Candidates' use of Twitter during the 2010 British and Dutch general election campaigns. *New Media & Society, 18*(5), 765–783.

Groves, R. M., Presser, S., & Dipko, S. (2004). The role of topic interest in survey participation decisions. *The Public Opinion Quarterly, 68*(1), 2–31.

Hall, J. L. (2008a). Improving the security, transparency, and efficiency of California's 1% manual tally procedures. *2008 USENIX/ACCURATE Electronic Voting Technology Workshop*. Retrieved from www.usenix.org/legacy/events/evt08/tech/full_papers/hall/hall.pdf

Hall, J. L. (2008b). Procedures for California's 1% manual tally. Retrieved from https://josephhall.org/procedures/ca_tally_procedures-2008.pdf

Hecht, B., Hong, L., Suh, B., & Chi, E. H. (2011). Tweets from Justin Bieber's heart: The dynamics of the location field in user profiles. In *Proceedings of the SIGCHI conference on human factors in computing systems* (pp. 237–246). New York, NY, USA: ACM.

Hernández, M. A., & Stolfo, S. J. (1995). The merge/purge problem for large databases. *ACM SIGMOD Record*, 24, pp. 127–138.

Herzog, T. N., Scheuren, F., & Winkler, W. E. (2010). Record linkage. *Wiley Interdisciplinary Reviews: Computational Statistics, 2*(5), 535–543.

Herzog, T. N., Scheuren, F. J., & Winkler, W. E. (2007). *Data quality and record linkage techniques*. Springer Science & Business Media.

Howard, P. N., Kollanyi, B., Bolsover, G., Bradshaw, S., & Neudert, L.-M. (2017). Junk news and bots during the US election: What were Michigan voters sharing over Twitter? *COMPROP Data Memo, 3*.

Ikawa, Y., Enoki, M., & Tatsubori, M. (2012). Location inference using microblog messages. In *Proceedings of the 21st international conference on world wide web* (pp. 687–690). New York, NY, USA: ACM.

Jaro, M. A. (1989). Advances in record-linkage methodology as applied to matching the 1985 census of Tampa, Florida. *Journal of the American Statistical Association, 84*(406), 414–420.

Key, V. O. (1984). *Southern politics in state and nation: A new edition*. The University of Tennessee Press.

Kim, S., Schneider, S., & Alvarez, R. M. (2019). Evaluating the quality of changes in voter registration databases. *American Politics Research*. doi: 10.1177/1532673X19870512

King, G., Lam, P., & Roberts, M. E. (2017). Computer-assisted keyword and document set discovery from unstructured text. *American Journal of Political Science, 61*(4), 971–988.

Klasnja, M., Barberá, P., Beauchamp, N., Nagler, J., & Tucker, J. (2018). Measuring public opinion with social media data. In L. R. Atkeson & R. M. Alvarez (Eds.), *The Oxford handbook of polling and survey methods*. Oxford University Press.

Kumar, S., Morstatter, F., & Liu, H. (2015). Analyzing Twitter data. In Y. Mejova, I. Weber, & M. W. Macy (Eds.), *Twitter: A digital socioscope* (pp. 21–51). Cambridge University Press.

Levenshtein, V. I. (1966). Binary codes capable of correcting deletions, insertions, and reversals. In *Soviet Physics Doklady*, 707–710.

Levin, I., Pomares, J., & Alvarez, R. M. (2016). Using machine learning algorithms to detect election fraud. In R. M. Alvarez (Ed.), *Computational social science: Discovery and prediction* (pp. 266–294). Cambridge University Press.

Li, C., & Sun, A. (2014). Fine-grained location extraction from tweets with temporal awareness. In *Proceedings of the 37th international ACM SIGIR conference on research & development in information retrieval* (pp. 43–52). New York, NY, USA: ACM.

Lin, Y., Keegan, B., Margolin, D., & Lazer, D. (2013). Rising tides or rising stars? Dynamics of shared attention on Twitter during media events. *CoRR, abs/1307.2785*. Retrieved from http://arxiv.org/abs/1307.2785

Lindeman, M., & Stark, P. B. (2012). A gentle introduction to risk-limiting audits. *IEEE Security and Privacy, Special Issue on Electronic Voting*. Retrieved from https://www.stat.berkeley.edu/~stark/Preprints/gentle12.pdf

Liu, A., Srikanth, M., Adams-Cohen, N., Alvarez, R. M., & Anandkumar, A. (2019). Finding social media trolls: Dynamic keyword selection methods for rapidly-evolving online debates. doi: http://dx.doi.org/abs/1911.05332

McGee, J., Caverlee, J., & Cheng, Z. (2013). Location prediction in social media based on tie strength. In *Proceedings of the 22nd ACM international conference on information & knowledge management* (pp. 459–468). New York, NY, USA: ACM.

McKinney, S. M., Houston, J. B., & Hawthorne, J. (2013). Social watching a 2012 Republican presidential primary debate. *American Behavioral Scientist, 58*, 556–573.

Mebane, W. R. (2008). Election forensics: The second-digit Benford's law test and recent American presidential elections. In R. M. Alvarez, T. E. Hall, & S. D. Hyde (Eds.), *Election fraud: Detecting and deterring electoral manipulation* (pp. 162–181). Brookings Institution Press.

Mebane, W. R. (2011). Comment on "Benford's law and the detection of election fraud." *Political Analysis, 19*(3), 269–272.

Montgomery, J. M., Olivella, S., Potter, J. D., & Crisp, B. F. (2015). An informed forensics approach to detecting vote irregularities. *Political Analysis, 23*(4), 488–505. doi: 10.1093/pan/mpv023

Murthy, D. (2015). Twitter and elections: Are tweets, predictive, reactive, or a form of buzz? *Information, Community & Society, 18*(7), 816–831.

Myakgov, M., Ordeshook, P. C., & Shaikin, D. (2009). *The forensics of election fraud.* Cambridge University Press.

Newcombe, H. B., Kennedy, J. M., Axford, S., & James, A. P. (1959). Automatic linkage of vital records. *Science, 130*, (3381) 954–959.

O'Connor, B., Balasubramanyan, R., & Routledge, B. R. (2010). From tweets to polls: Linking text sentiment to public opinion time series. In *Proceedings of the fourth international AAAI conference on weblogs and social media.* Washington, DC: AAAI.

Orange County Registrar of Voters. (2018). *Register to vote, or change your name, address or party.* Retrieved from `www.ocvote.com/registration/register-to-vote/`

Orange County Registrar of Voters. (2019). *Orange county registrar of voters 2018 risk limiting audit pilot project report.* Retrieved from `https://bit.ly/2YYTBbX`

Roberts, M. E., Stewart, B. M., Tingley, D., et al. (2014). Structural topic models for open-ended survey responses. *American Journal of Political Science, 58*(4), 1064–1082. doi: 10.1111/ajps.12103

Rozenas, A. (2017). Detecting election fraud from irregularities in vote-share distributions. *Political Analysis, 25*(1), 41–56. doi: 10.1017/pan.2016.9

Sajuria, J., & Fabrega, J. (2016). Do we need polls? Why Twitter will not replace opinion surveys, but can complement them. In H. Snee, C. Hine, Y. Morey, S. Roberts, & H. Watson (Eds.), *Digital methods for social science: An interdisciplinary guide to research innovation* (pp. 87–104). Palgrave Macmillan.

Särndal, C.-E., & Lundström, S. (2005). *Estimation in surveys with nonresponse.* John Wiley & Sons.

Schuman, H., & Presser, S. (1996). *Questions and answers in attitude surveys: Experiments on question form, wording, and context.* SAGE Publications.

Selker, T. (2005). Election auditing is an end-to-end procedure. *Science, 308*(5730), 1873–1874.

Stark, P. B. (2009). Risk-limiting postelection audits: Conservative p-values from common probability inequalities. *IEEE Transactions on Information Forensics and Security, 4*(4), 1005–1014.

Steinert-Threkeld, Z. C. (2018). *Twitter as data.* Cambridge University Press.

Theocharis, Y., Barberá, P., Fazekas, Z., Popa, S. A., & Parnet, O. (2016). A bad workman blames his tweets: The consequences of citizens' uncivil Twitter. *Journal of Communication, 66*(6), 1007–1031.

Vallis, O., Hochenbaum, J., & Kejariwal, A. (2014). A novel technique for long-term anomaly detection in the cloud. In *6th USENIX Workshop on Hot Topics in Cloud Computing (HotCloud 14).* Philadelphia, PA. Retrieved from `www.usenix.org/conference/hotcloud14/workshop-program/presentation/vallis`

Vosoughi, S. (2015). *Automatic detection and verification of rumors on Twitter.* Ph.D. Thesis, Massachusetts Institute of Technology.

Williams, V. (2018, November 29). Lawsuit by Abrams PAC continues debate over voter suppression in bitter Georgia governor's race. *The Washington Post.* Retrieved from `www.washingtonpost.com/politics/lawsuit-alleges-voter-suppression-in-bitter-georgia-governors`

`-race-and-seeks-protections-for-future-races/2018/11/29/`
`750afc20-f353-11e8-aeea-b85fd44449f5_story.html`

Winkler, W. E. (1988). Using the em algorithm for weight computation in the Fellegi–Sunter model of record linkage. In *Proceedings of the section on survey research methods, American Statistical Association* (Vol. 667, p. 671).

Winkler, W. E. (1990). String comparator metrics and enhanced decision rules in the Fellegi–Sunter model of record linkage. In *Proceedings of the Section on Survey Research Methods* American Statistical Association. (pp. 354–359).

Winkler, W. E., & Thibaudeau, Y. (1991). An application of the Fellegi–Sunter model of record linkage to the 1990 US Decennial Census. *US Bureau of the Census*, 1–22.

Yancey, W. E. (2005). *Evaluating string comparator performance for record linkage*. Technical Report RR2005/05, US Bureau of the Census.

Zhang, M., Alvarez, R. M., & Levin, I. (2019). Election forensics: Using machine learning and synthetic data for possible election anomaly detection. *PLoS ONE, 14*. doi: http://dx.doi.org/10.1371/journal.pone .0223950

Acknowledgments

A project like this cannot be successfully conducted without a lot of advice, input, and assistance. First of all, we thank Neal Kelley, the Orange County Registrar of Voters, for his collaboration with us on this project. Neal's advice, enthusiasm, and interest in using data to improve the election process in Orange County provided the foundation for our project. Working with academic researchers is not easy, and Neal's willingness to collaborate with us, his patience with our requests, and his comments and critiques of our work, were important for our success. We also thank Justin Berardino of the OCROV for his help – Justin, the OCROV's Operations Manager, played a crucial role in helping us with data and information about elections in Orange County.

Second, we thank the John Randolph Haynes and Dora Haynes Foundation, which provided funding for this project. The mission of the Haynes Foundation is to support social science research, especially in Southern California. They have long provided financial support for research that seeks to improve a social scientific understanding of California's unique democracy, and we hope that our research reported in this Element contributes to that same understanding.

Third, a number of people have helped us with this research project. Sabrina Hameister at Caltech assisted with project logistics, and we could not have easily run this project without her help. A number of Caltech students participated in this research project, and we thank them for their assistance: Jack Briones, Ethan Eason, Daniel Guth, Claire Ho, Joanna Huey, Michelle Hyun, Cheria Jia, Nailen Matschke, Matt Riker, and Spencer Schneider. Academic colleagues provided comments and advice at various stages in this project, and we thank Lonna Atkeson, Paul Gronke, Thad Hall, Jonathan Katz, Ines Levin, Paul Manson, and Charles Stewart for their support and advice.

Some of the research reported here has been presented at research conferences and workshops, especially our work on voter registration database auditing: We thank participants at the 2018 Southern California Methods Conference (especially Steven Liao), and Election Audit Summit held at MIT, December 7–8, 2018. The registration auditing project was also presented at the 2019 Annual Meeting of the Midwest Political Science Association, the Election Sciences, Reform, and Administration 2019 conference, and the 2019

Annual Meeting of the Society for Political Methodology – we thank participants from those conferences for their comments and questions. We presented some of the material from this project at the "Election Administration and Technology Symposium," hosted by the Bedrosian Center at the USC Sol Price School of Public Policy; we thank Jeff Jenkins for inviting us, and for hosting the symposium, and of course we thank the symposium participants for their comments on our work.

Finally, code and data from our research are available on our project's GitHub (https://github.com/monitoringtheelection). Due to the ongoing nature of this project, and the sensitive nature of some of the data, only certain datasets and code will be available on the GitHub. Researchers who are interested in data or code that is not on the project GitHub are encouraged to contact the authors.

Cambridge Elements ☰

Elements in Campaigns and Elections

R. Michael Alvarez
California Institute of Technology
R. Michael Alvarez is Professor of Political and Computational Social Science at Caltech. His current research focuses on election administration and technology, campaigns and elections, and computational modeling.

Emily Beaulieu Bacchus
University of Kentucky
Emily Beaulieu Bacchus is Associate Professor of Political Science and Director of International Studies at the University of Kentucky. She is an expert in political institutions and contentious politics—focusing much of her work on perceptions of election fraud and electoral protests. *Electoral Protest and Democracy in the Developing World* was published with Cambridge University Press in 2014.

Charles Stewart III
Massachusetts Institute of Technology
Charles Stewart III is the Kenan Sahin Distinguished Professor of Political Science at MIT. His research and teaching focus on American politics, election administration, and legislative politics.

About the Series
Broadly focused, covering electoral campaigns & strategies, voting behavior, and electoral institutions, this Elements series offers the opportunity to publish work from new and emerging fields, especially those at the interface of technology, elections, and global electoral trends.

We seek authoritative manuscripts and cutting edge work on electoral institutions and the administration of elections; election and campaign technology; political campaign strategy, tactics, and communications; campaign finance and spending; polling, surveying, and predictive modeling for political campaigns; participation in politics and turnout; voting behavior; emotions, political, and cognitive psychology; and voter mobilization. While much of the work in this field is quantitative or formal/game-theoretic in nature, we encourage submissions that use multiple methods, including qualitative methodologies and creative ways of integrating empirics. For quantitative research, we will seek to integrate data and code into published manuscripts; and for mixed or qualitative methods, we will work on creative ways of integrating empirical data such as images, interview texts or recordings, or archival documents.

Cambridge Elements ≡

Elements in Campaigns and Elections

Elements in the Series

Securing American Elections: How Data-Driven Election Monitoring Can Improve Our Democracy
R. Michael Alvarez, Nicholas Adams-Cohen,
Seo-Young Silvia Kim and Yimeng Li

A full series listing is available at: www.cambridge.org/EPEC

Printed in the United States
By Bookmasters